The THRIVE© Approach
To Mental Wellness
Marion Aslan & Mike Smith
2007

Building your resilience and finding your future

The THRIVETM Approach to Mental Wellness

By Marion Aslan & Mike Smith

Copyright Marion Aslan & Mike Smith, 2007
Published by crazy diamond 2007

www.crazydiamond.org.uk

British Library Cataloguing in Publication Data
A catalogue record for this book is available from The British Library

ISBN 978-0-9556461-0-2

Printed and bound in England by Clifford Press Ltd, Coventry

It is a great privilege and pleasure to be asked to write a foreword for THRIVE which for me is not just any book. THRIVE speaks to me in one of those rare, powerful and deep ways and touches my soul as the psychiatric survivor that I am. However THRIVE will not just appeal to those who have had psychic distress in their lives. It goes beyond that.

By using the words psychic distress rather than many of the words bandied about by the psychiatric system and picked up in the general public this book is making a statement. A statement fashioned by the authors' alternative viewpoints on the psyche and the distress people can experience due to life experiences. The statement is power, your power, the power that exists within all of us to make choices about who you are and how you choose to live your life regardless of the almost insurmountable difficulties one might have encountered in life. THRIVE gives you the tools for finding this intrinsic power which exists within each of us and the inspiration to take up the challenge.

It does this by looking at the six elements which make up THRIVE; *time, healing, resilience, interdependence, vivacity and emancipation.* Six elements which though very different are so connected that together they send a reverberating message to all who should choose to read this book. I cannot imagine that anyone who reads this book will not come away from it without feeling inspired or invigorated or more knowledgeable on the elements that can hinder or encourage personal growth. Neither can I imagine anyone coming away from this book without the feeling that they have smelled the scent of freedom or the rainbow of possibilities that lie stretched out before them.

Olga Runciman, Chair Danish Hearing Voices Network

"Remember when you were young, you shone like the sun
Shine on you crazy diamond
Now there's a look in your eyes, like black holes in the sky
Shine on you crazy diamond"
Pink Floyd
In memorium Syd Barrett and all those crazy diamonds taken too soon

This book is dedicated to Chris Rankin and John Williams

The THRIVE© Approach to mental wellness - An alternative concept

Many people experience severe psychic distress at some point in their life - 1 in 4 of us in the course of a year according to statistics, and at the time it can be totally devastating. Quite apart from the distress this causes to the individual and their loved ones, some people report feeling misunderstood and even frightened by a society which often focuses on illness, deficits, losses and stigmatisation. Many myths and misconceptions still abound regarding mental ill health - not only those held by the general public, but ironically sometimes by those working within mental health systems.

Very often the emphasis is on mental ill health rather than wellness, problems rather than skills, symptoms rather than resilience, and despite the concept of recovery being recognised, helping agencies remain predominantly singularly medical in approach and more target driven than people orientated. Sometimes workers feel disempowered, lack confidence or don't fully understand what it is that nurtures recovery.

The THRIVE© approach takes a more positive stance. Devised by Mike Smith, a nurse of 25 years experience and former Director of Nursing in North Birmingham and Marion Aslan, a former user of mental health services who has worked in the learning disabilities and mental health voluntary sector for the last 30 years, we have drawn on our experiences of what keeps people maintained within the system and what works in the moving on process, whereby people thrive and find their future.

If at the moment you are struggling with emotional problems you may feel as if no one could possibly understand what you've been through, how it feels and the degree of pain or even worse, "nothingness" that you experience. It is possible, however, to assist yourself to move beyond being someone who is "maintained" by the system to someone who is emancipated from being regarded as an "ill" person and who can thrive; someone who can derive pleasure from life again, able to meet life's challenges.

Several years ago, like so many others I have met, I was told by one psychiatrist that I had a severe and enduring mental health problem, would need to take medication for the rest of my life and should consider whether working full or even part time would be too stressful. Just to complete the total demolition of my life, it was suggested that as I had had a recent car accident I should give up driving.

The journey back to wellness, happiness and emancipation hasn't always been easy but it certainly hasn't been insurmountable, nor "impossible" as that psychiatrist implied, and that seems to hold true for many survivors of the system. There are common themes and stages of survival which we have documented here collectively as the THRIVE© approach, along with some useful person centred planning tools to help you on your journey towards emancipation.

Marion Aslan 2007

This approach is about drawing together a philosophy and conviction of hope and growth in a systematic way which will help you to reform your current experiences into a more helpful one that can lead you forward, it is aimed at people who are looking for someway of reclaiming what they believe is their true path and finding sanity in a somewhat disordered world.

The concept of THRIVE© is one of taking the key themes of restoration and recovery and using them as the foundation stones for finding and achieving the future you want to build. The six themes are each described at the beginnings of their chapters and if you read around the area of personal growth and survival you will see these themes emerging as we did from the experiences of others who have trodden the path.

These themes are not linear; you do not have to go from one to the other. Rather, when considered together they show a general approach or map by which peoples recovery journeys meander.

If recovery is a journey, a process, a direction rather than an event or a label then there has to be a map, a guide, short cuts, beginnings and an overall direction, we hope to guide you on your recovery and if nothing else, we hope you enjoy the view on the way.

Mike Smith 2007

You reached for the secret too soon, you cried for the moon
Shine on you crazy diamond
Threatened by shadows at night, and exposed in the light
Shine on you crazy diamond

Well you wore out your welcome with random precision
Rode on the steel breeze
Come on you raver, you seer of visions
Come on you painter, you piper, you prisoner and shine!
Pink Floyd "Shine on you crazy diamond"

Introduction
The THRIVE© Approach
Building resilience and finding your future

Recovery following distressing experiences can be a seemingly complicated phenomenon that is described in complex language by many people. In reality however there are a number of underpinning focal elements that are the foundations for personal recovery and moving on to find a future and build your resilience. For comfort and ease of navigation we refer to these underpinnings collectively as THRIVE©. They come in no particular order, have no greater merits than as a descriptor and are no more or less important than each other. We are not going to debate here the academic background or validity for the work, suffice to say that the proof of the pudding is in the eating.

THRIVE© - The 6 underpinning factors of recovery/survival and mental wellness -

> **Time**
> **Healing**
> **Resilience**
> **Interdependence**
> **Vivacity**
> **Emancipation**

We have devoted chapters to each of these themes with ideas for self support and moving on, some of our own thoughts and experiences, a number of exercises to gauge where you are in your recovery, some positive words of encouragement, and some relevant poetry and song lyrics that you may enjoy.

For ease of navigating your way through (you may, like us, prefer to flick through some books rather than read cover to cover!) the practical exercises and questions that you may find useful are in blue print. Use them as thinking points or if you prefer you could use a notebook to record your answers.

Where possible, though, we suggest you discuss your responses with a trusted supporter – that could be a friend, a family member, good neighbour - anyone who has your best interests at heart. Using the notion that a problem shared is a problem halved you may find talking to someone in this way very therapeutic. If you prefer, however, simply make time for yourself to reflect and come to your own judgements. Most importantly, don't give up hope, all things must pass!

"A cloudburst doesn't last all day"   *George Harrison "All things must pass"*

"In brightest day or darkest night
Don't give up the faith
Keep your heart right
Like the mountains stand for eternity
Your light will shine for all to see"

> *Terry Callier - "Keep your heart right"*

Chapter 1
The THRIVE© Approach
Getting started

Does it feel as if there are just too many difficulties in your life for you to move on? Do you feel that there's nothing to hope for in the future?

Do any of these sound familiar?
"I can't do things because of my illness"
"I try but don't get anywhere, so what's the point of trying?"
"I don't know where to start"

It can be very frustrating when you are feeling low, and you see other people around you who seem to be enjoying and getting on with their lives. It can make you depressed just to see positivity and success in others when you feel that your life is in turmoil, as it can serve to throw a torchlight onto your own life. To think about building your resilience and finding a better future might seem a distant dream at the moment and particularly so if you are anxious or depressed.

Whilst many people experience depression from time to time as a reaction to events or situations, for some people it can become totally debilitating and cause ongoing problems by affecting day to day functioning and how you respond to other people. Motivation goes out of the window, lethargy creeps in and you can't be bothered to change things – what's the point? Life's a bitch, and then you die!

Or do you need to turn your thinking around? This is what we call the ability to reframe and reform your experiences. Sometimes by learning to think differently about ourselves, our situation and others around us, we are able to overcome the debilitative aspects of our lives and work towards a more positive future.

For example, it can often feel as if your glass is half empty. Or is it half full! Maybe neither of these is correct!

The reality may be an alternative way of thinking. Maybe the glass isn't big enough or you are drinking too quickly! This is what we mean by reforming your experiences into a potentially more helpful one. There are many ways of looking at a situation, maybe you just need to consider the different choices available to you.

Cycles of thinking

This may require looking at your current "cycles" of thinking, and making a determined effort to change or reshape them. Are you caught up in a cycle of despair and negativity? Mind, body and spirit are interlinked. If negativity and depression prevail this has an adverse effect on each of those.

Positive emotions such as happiness serve to improve physical, psychological and emotional wellbeing. Therefore by changing how we think or act we can reduce the levels of anxiety and work towards a healthier mind, body and spirit. Alternatively we can remain going round and round in circles, becoming increasingly frustrated, more depressed and despondent and sink further and further into mental ill health. Mental wellness requires change!

The basics of Cognitive Behavioural Therapy are something we can all learn to do for ourselves.

Cognitive = How we think

Behaviour = How we act

By *changing* how we think or act we can reduce the level of anxiety

Any change is difficult. But change is possible and this manual is intended to help you identify the changes you want to make in your life and offer choices for improving on how things currently are. This is no quick fix cure, and it requires effort and hard work. Rather it is about framing your own understanding of your experiences, becoming more confident and able to vocalise what you really want from others and from yourself.

Maybe your current distress is as a result of past events or the actions of other people. You may have accepted that you can't change the past, other people or everything around you, (and that is a giant milestone to reach in itself) but it can still be difficult to let go of feelings of anger, overwhelm, frustration and bitterness. Although you can't change the past, you can change how you feel about the past and your hopefulness for the future. This manual may help you to explore that further.

By building up your confidence, self esteem and understanding of yourself and your experiences this will empower you to move towards health and focus more on what you want to do and be. Initially emotional difficulties may seem limiting but this does not necessarily have to be the case. Many people who have been diagnosed even with severe mental health problems have gone on not only to recover, but to thrive and reclaim their lives. Hence the title of our approach, THRIVE©

The THRIVE© Approach recognises that people often end up where they are emotionally as a result of childhood or past trauma and there may be specific issues that are causing you distress. Often the medical system ignores these issues, concentrating instead on the way you cope and calling them the symptoms of an illness, e.g. Self Harm. Because of this society has developed entire constructs of illness based upon pathologising peoples distress and efforts to survive. It is one way of seeing the world, however it is a not very helpful one for the person at the centre, resulting in illness and loss of hope at best.

Rather than talk about mental illness we prefer to use the terminology psychic distress, i.e. distress relating to the mind. These psychic experiences need to be seen as what they are, not symptoms but consequences of events and experiences.

Hurting yourself for example is not a symptom of a disorder nor is it ever THE problem for some people. Rather, it is the solution at that time; it is a method of survival, understanding and communicating with the wide world we live in. If you explore how people survive and grow, recognising these things can sometimes take years. Giving up the labels and finding a future has taken many strong people years to attain; we aim to try to speed it up a little for you by offering you the THRIVE© approach.

In order to thrive, there is a clear process which embraces recovery but goes even further and liberates the individual. It can be actively supported by friends, family, workers and colleagues, but the key person is you, your hopes and desires and a commitment to reclaiming your life.

There is nothing wrong in asking for help, indeed it's something we may not do often enough! But it is important to recognise that people are there to facilitate your recovery, they can't do it for you. It is your responsibility to determine your path and inform others of the nature of the help you require. It is equally the responsibility of your supporters to listen to what you require and support by doing with and enabling rather than doing for and disabling.

Clouds are not the cheeks of angels you know
They're only clouds, friendly sometimes
But you can never be sure
If I had longer arms I'd push the clouds away
Or make them hang above the water somewhere else
But I'm just a man who needs and wants, mostly things he'll never have
Looking for that thing that's hardest to find – himself

I've been going a long time now
Along the way I've learned some things
You have to make the good times yourself
Take the little times and make them into big times
And save the times that are alright
For the ones that aren't so good
I've never been able to push the clouds away by myself
Help me
Please   *Rod McKuen "Pushing the clouds away"*

Remember, people DO recover from mental health problems and the terms Schizophrenia, Personality Disorder, Bi-polar Disorder etc. are just labels used to describe a set of problems in your life; they don't define who you are!! And they certainly need not dictate the course of your life!

These labels used by the medical profession and others are mostly harmful because it is a poor description of the experience that says nothing of its origins or solutions. You may have little in common with other people with the same label, it has little scientific validity and most importantly says nothing about the origin of the experience nor how to put things right.

People who have had the experience of hearing voices, becoming psychotic, self harming or being severely depressed and anxious all have one thing in common. As they move on in recovery they find that they are more in control, rather than allowing themselves to be controlled. Some people may not stop self harming, they may continue to hear voices and to feel down – the key is for them to be able to live life well regardless of these things.

Learning for yourself how to deal with your distress is far more important than being taught what to do. That is not to say that interventions and support from mental health professionals are not relevant at all, and support may be an essential element of your recovery, but the role of supporter should be one of mutuality and reciprocity. You are the key person, the one guiding the process – your supporter is there as an encourager of recovery.

Hope and optimism, as we'll see later, is also crucial to the process and even this can be learned!
It is understandable that psychic distress and how others respond to this distress, can lead to us thinking in negative ways about the future, and such negative thinking can make all sorts of things incredibly difficult. It is like a leak in your confidence bucket - constantly drip-drip-dripping away your confidence and self esteem.

There is a degree of skill and commitment to moving away from the person who sees the glass permanently as half empty to the person who sees it as half full! You CAN move from being stuck to someone who is in control. A starting point might be to consider a different way of looking at your situation (glass not big enough) and firstly remember that it is not permanent. It will pass.

By accepting that it is only temporary, some people are able to nurture and develop a positive mental attitude – positive thinking. Positive thinking is a mental attitude that sees the bright side of life and focuses on the full half of the glass and not on the empty half.

It is a mental attitude that expects positive results. People with a positive frame of mind think about possibilities, growth, expansion and success. They expect happiness, health, love and good relationships. They think in terms of 'I can', 'I am able' and 'I will succeed'.

The good news is that if you have picked up this manual you are interested in moving on, getting your life back, recovering. And there exists already that seed of hope.

"Today you are living in winter.
Trust that spring will come"
Jean Vanier

Chapter 2
The THRIVE© Approach
The 6 underpinning factors
THRIVE © Time, Healing, Resilience, Interdependence, Vivacity, Emancipation

TIME is a natural healer as long as we don't resist the process and become stuck. Think of someone you have loved who has died. The pain of grief becomes less raw over time – you don't forget or stop missing the person, but over time you focus on the joy of knowing them rather than the pain of losing them. So it can be with emotional problems. With TIME you will feel differently, gain a different perspective and move away from the distress you feel right now.

HEALING is integral to recovery and essential to everyone's wellbeing, sometimes easier to impart to others than to give to ourselves. There may be reasons why we block our own healing – guilt, worthlessness, shame, lack of belief in our own worth. Part of the healing process is to acknowledge these emotions, and allow healing elements into our consciousness.

Showing **RESILIENCE** is a common factor in those who have survived and rebuilt their lives. Indeed we all have a degree of resilience, and some people are able to draw on their inner reserves and show resilience even where the system attempts to squash it. It is also possible to build up our own resilience and to help support the process in others.

Often people make the mistake of striving for total independence. This is not realistic – we all rely on other people for some things some of the time, and other people may rely on us. A healthier attitude is to look at ways of increasing our personal connections and relationships, building circles of **INTERDEPENDENCE** also as we say above many people are great at helping others and being strong allies and supporters for others, not as good when it comes to themselves.

VIVACITY is not a term we hear very often in mental health spheres, (you might be mistaken for being manic?) but our conviction is that we should be thinking about this as a vital part of recovery. Having a lust for life, being animated, full of enjoyment of living is possible for all. Many people who have experienced severe lows in their lives talk about enjoying life even more after coming through illness or depression. The friendships you forge in adversity tend to be based on mutual respect, affection and consideration, and as the saying goes, "All that doesn't kill us makes us grow".

EMANCIPATION or liberation comes with taking control of one's own life and celebrating your own individuality and uniqueness. Playing a vital role in society and being valued can enhance our sense of freedom and remove us from the constraints of being regarded as mentally unwell, maintained in the system and feeling life happens to other people. It is a club for which you don't have to keep membership fees going!!

As Groucho Marx puts it,
"Please accept my resignation. I don't want to belong to any club that will accept me as a member"

Groucho Marx 1895 –1977; Groucho and Me (1959)

Chapter 3
The THRIVE© Approach
Moving Forward

"Nothing is permanent. Everything is in a continual state of change, movement. Nothing lasts forever except the life force itself"

Carol Jerrems, Australian photographer

Moving forward

There is a famous saying, "The journey of a thousand miles starts with a single step"
Our take on that is if you're still standing, you're already on the journey! And given the life stories and experiences of some people we meet it is admirable they have survived thus far. Maybe your experiences have also been traumatic, painful and difficult to deal with. With support, self nurturing and mentoring you can become resilient even in the face of adversity. It's ok to take small steps at a time, and even to retreat at times. It's also ok to get angry at events or people who have caused you pain. This manual will enable you to explore that anger and many other emotions.

Maybe you are feeling overwhelmed - thoughts, feelings, ideas and emotions jumbled and confused. This manual can be "dipped into" rather than fully digested, so don't worry if you're already struggling with taking it all in. Come back to it as and when you wish, turn to any page! Hopefully there will be something to inspire! Sometimes life can bring us to places where we just need to stop, take a deep breath, and gather our strength to make it through just one more day.
Take a moment to relax, enjoy and reflect on the messages in the songs, affirmations and poetry.

"All the places I've been make it hard to begin
To enjoy life again on the inside, but I mean to.
Take a walk in the park,
Does the wind in the dark sound like music to you?
Well I'm thinking it does to me.

"Inside" - JethroTull

What or who might prevent you from moving on?
It may be that you feel "stuck" and there is little hope that the future can bring anything rewarding or positive. Maybe you struggle to "get through" the day and feel that this is as good as it gets. Maybe that's what others have told you!

There are many examples of people diagnosed with severe mental illness who have decided to give up or even challenge the label and get on with their lives. Consider the following quote from Judi Chamberlain, now working with the National Empowerment Centre in America

> *"Well, I've been a good patient and I've been a bad patient, and, believe me, being a good patient helps to get you out of the hospital, but being a bad patient helps to get you back to real life"*

The THRIVE© Approach firmly believes that the individual is the expert of his or her own experiences, and within every person lies the necessary resources to facilitate reclamation of their life. No one is an island and some help may be necessary – that may be a worker you trust or a friend or family member.

What is essential is that you determine the pace and how you use this book, and that the help and support you require is determined and directed by you.

There is no right or wrong way to use this book. So dip in where you wish, answer the questions only if you want to – simply enjoy the photographs – see if you recognise the song lyrics! Get angry at it and use that anger as energy. But whichever, whatever, however - we hope you enjoy it, catch a glimpse of your strengthened future and thrive!

Do I want to move on?

This is not as absurd as it sounds. There are many reasons why it is easier, safer and preferable to stay put rather than move on. The social system can be very paternalistic which in turn encourages us to be childlike, dependent and fearful of anything different. Even our benefit systems create "madness - financial dependency" so it is not surprising that often moving on seems just too difficult, lacking in real rewards and unrealistic. However it is well documented by those who have recovered that the benefits outweigh the difficulties of the journey. Do you want to move on?

Take a few minutes to complete the following. It may help you to identify where you are now, and the reasons you feel helpless to move on. You might prefer to answer the questions in private or you might wish to ask someone you trust to help you as it can be useful to get another viewpoint.

Answer agree, disagree or don't know to the following questions

1. You would like to move on and reclaim your life, but often end up doing what you feel is expected of you?
2. Are you always trying to please other people?
3. As you recover, are people more demanding of you?
4. As you recover are there difficulties in relating to people in a different way?
5. Are you trying to break the cycle of illness but not actually finding alternative sources of pleasure?
6. As you recover do you feel you have the skills for coping with other people's demands?
7. Do you have some fear of change?
8. Do you expect and fear any degree of failure?
9. Do you have a fear of the future because it is unknown?
10. Do you feel there was some "Safety" in the past, even where there was trauma?
11. Are you comfortable with "today" and just making it through the day?
12. Have you begun to accept that "this is as good as it gets"?
13. Would the effort to move on and be a different person be too painful?
14. Would the effort to move on and emancipate yourself be hard work?"
15. Are there issues in your past, maybe violence, guilt or abuse that prevents you moving on?
16. Do you feel you lack the support of other people to assist you moving on?

If possible, talk through the above with someone you trust and who cares about you. It may help you build up your understanding of where you are and the challenges to be faced.

What support do you feel that you need in your life in order to move on?
Who, realistically, do you wish to give you that support?

See the possibilities in the new and do not be paralyzed by the difficulties to be overcome

"It is never too late to be what you might have been"
George Eliot

Affirmations

Some people find that starting each day with an affirmation or positive saying helps get them motivated and ready for the journey of recovery. It gets you accustomed to saying or thinking optimistically.

Write one of the following out and place it on the fridge or a mirror.
Start each day repeating it several times.

Better still; think of some of your own! They could be lines from songs or poems that mean something to you. It doesn't matter at this stage if you believe the affirmations, it's enough just to say them, and try to do so out loud. Most of us feel awkward saying positive things about ourselves, but it will encourage you to look at things in a slightly different way, thus aiding the recovery process.

"My analyst told me that I was right out of my head
The way he described it he said Id be better dead than live
I didn't listen to his jive
I knew all along that he was all wrong
And I knew that he thought I was crazy but I'm not
Oh no"

Joni Mitchell "Twisted"

"Success should be measured not so much by the position one has reached in life as by the obstacles which one has overcome while trying to succeed"

"Discover a sense of mission that life may be important and purposeful for you rather then dull and purposeless"

"Never accept the negative until you have fully explored the positive"

"When it is dark enough, you can see the stars"

www.worldlandtrust.org

Chapter 4
The THRIVE© Approach
Time

"Ticking away the moments that make up a dull day
You fritter and waste the hours in an off hand way
Kicking around on a piece of ground in your home town
Waiting for someone or something to show you the way
Pink Floyd "Time"

There are contradictory opinions as to whether time in itself is a healing force, as illustrated in the following two quotes

"Time has too much credit…it is not a great healer. It is an indifferent and perfunctory one. Sometimes it does not heal at all. And sometimes when it seems to, no healing has been necessary"
Ivy Compton-Burnett 1884 -1969 "Darkness and Day"

"Time is the great physician"
Benjamin Disraeli 1804 – 1881 "Henrietta Temple"

Time may not be helpful as a healer for all, but you do have to allow time to heal and you must not allow yourself to be stuck in time when chronological time is flowing over you.

Maybe it's not particularly useful for you to think in these terms at all! Often we put our own pressures and expectations on ourselves, using time as a benchmark or a target. Our view is that recovery occurs at your own individual pace and at the right time for you! There will be a right time to disclose, to take responsibility and the right time to move on. Certainly, space, distance and time from the event give us the ability to make sense of what has happened and put it into context. This will lead to moving on. Another useful way of regarding time, then, is as described in the biblical passage from Ecclesiastes or the song by the Byrds!

"To everything there is a season, and a time to every purpose under the heaven;
A time to be born and a time to die; a time to plant, and a time to pluck up that which is planted;
A time to weep, and a time to laugh; a time to mourn, and a time to dance"

If we take this more pragmatic view and see recovery, like life itself as a journey we may accept that there is always a beginning, however, many journeys have no end as such (or we keep taking new routes!) so just enjoy the travelling, you may be on the road for some considerable time!

"For me, as for many people, I think of Recovery from mental ill health as a journey. On the way I have met wonderful companions who enhanced that journey and have had support from a range of people at various stages of the journey. This has allowed me to 'chart my own course' and enjoy each part of the journey as an adventure in itself, and equate the journey of recovery with the journey of life itself! Therefore if things go badly, I can somehow keep a bigger picture and see it as part of life's rich tapestry rather than a signal that I am 'unwell'. Marion

Reaching a turning point

A turning point is reported by most people as a first and clear step in their recovery.

"A clear turning point may be a result of an event or an individual's inspiration which results in you resolving to move on and determining to conquer barriers to you living your life".

Topor et al (1998)

Turning points can occur at any time in our lives and can be minor or major experiences. Often it is only in retrospect that we recognise them as key events. Meeting someone new, changing jobs, moving house, a phone call, a letter or just having a change of mind may prove to be a critical turning point for some people.

There is often no knowing when, how, where these things will happen but they do regardless of how well or unwell we are. Simply by being aware that they can happen may help you to recognise them for what they are – milestones on your journey.

The 5 step process for reformation – your milestones
- **Reaching a turning point**
- **Identifying your experiences**
- **Exploring them in depth**
- **Understanding & organising your experiences in a way that is helpful to you**
- **Moving on**

1. Reaching a turning point
- **Be positive and hopeful**
- **Get angry, get constructive**
- **Own the experience and the recovery**
- **Look outwards and look within**
- **Don't wait for a coming wonder**
- **Be active**
- **Recruit allies and support**
- **Have a broad vision**
- **Understand the theories**
- **Meet with others**
- **Plan to deal with crises and emergencies**

2. Identifying your experiences

Identifying and forming a clear view in your own language about what your experiences actually have been, how they have changed, when they happened and what were the effects upon you.

- **What are they?**
- **When did they start?**
- **How does it affect your life?**
- **How does it relate to your life experiences directly/indirectly?**
- **Life histories**
- **Where are you in your experience? Startled, frightened, organising etc.**
- **What is your personal experience, not your label?**

3. Exploring your experiences in depth

Exploring in depth why and how you have become distressed including any things that trigger your current experiences, relating it beyond yourself to your social system such as the responses of mental health services.

- **What has helped?**
- **What hinders?**
- **Who helps?**
- **Links. Is your depression related to anything in your life?**
- **Can you do anything about this? Do you want to?**

4. Understanding and organizing your experiences

- **What are your beliefs or frame of reference for your experience?**
- **How have they changed?**
- **Look outward – what are the links. What went before?**
- **Who is around to help you and who has helped in the past?**
- **What are your fears? What are your dreams?**
- **What do you want?**
- **How can you deal with them?**
- **Can you be strategic?**
- **How can you have more control**
- **What are the real problems for you? Is it depression or is it your fears?**

5. Moving On

- **What do you want? What will help you?**
- **What coping mechanisms can you learn?**
- **Can you resolve or accept any past issues in your life that are significant?**
- **Where can you get the things that can help?**
- **What can mental health services do to help you?**
- **How can you develop alliances?**
- **How can you cope with the things that get in the way?**
- **Where do you want to go?**
- **How can you cope, be less distressed, not functionally impaired?**
- **What treatments/ approaches do you want to try?**
- **Who have been and will be your guides?**
- **Plan for crises**
- **Treatment plans and predetermination**

People as turning points

Sometimes it takes just one person to make us see things differently, influence us or support us. That person may be the turning point – the time when you "turn a corner" and your life changes albeit in small ways. There is a saying, "As one door closes, another opens" and this can be very helpful to remember. Many people we know who have experienced mental health problems would acknowledge that although they may have preferred to forgo the experience, there have been some compensations – usually in the form of people they have met, experiences gained and the wisdom often gained from rising from despondency.

Events as the turning point

Sometimes taking up a new activity or joining a club of some sort is the catalyst for change, as it can increase confidence and offers the opportunity to meet different people. If things have become routine and boring it is easy to dwell on your mental health problems. Going somewhere or doing something e.g. visiting the museum / art gallery or going for a long walk may not radically change your life but at least it occupies a chunk of time meaningfully, prevents you getting in a negative cycle and there is always the possibility of something interesting happening!

Many people have spoken about the positive effect on their own mental health of helping others – it detracts from your problems and gives a wider perspective. Have you considered doing a couple of hours voluntary work? It can give you experience and also increases self worth as you feel others value you.

Self as the turning point

The biggest obstacle or the biggest help can be ourselves. It can be easy to sink into depression, to become isolated, introspective and lethargic. Far easier to become reclusive, watch T.V. all day or stay in bed than to face the day and make it an interesting one. It may be that you need to retreat and do just that occasionally. At times the best healing may arise from being able to shut yourself off from the strains and stresses of everyday life and just give yourself quiet time. The danger is if you let that carry on, day after day, you end up putting yourself into a prison- like situation.

Depression and Suicide

The hopelessness associated with depression is the most common reason why someone may have thoughts of suicide and most suicides are linked to depression in some way. But there are things that you can do, as this book will explain, to help you fight feelings of depression and find ways not only of coping but of reclaiming your enjoyment of life.

- Remain connected to people and the world around you
- Find hope
- Find something to do each day that will take your mind off negative thoughts
- Get some exercise, maybe go for a walk or cycle ride
- Spend at least half an hour outside each day in the fresh air
- Avoid sleeping during the day if possible – if you are awake at night problems may seem worse!
- Excess alcohol or drugs may alleviate problems initially but may make you more depressed in the long run
- Breathing exercises may prove useful – there are some later in the book

If thoughts of suicide become more prevalent talk to someone non judgemental, phone the Samaritans, get help to reframe your thinking.

"Depression is a prison which we build for ourselves.
Just as we build it, so we can unlock the door and let ourselves out"
              Dorothy Rowe – "Depression, the Way out of your Prison"

Once you understand that you do not have to remain in the prison you can start looking outwards and think about venturing out. That is when you become your own turning point!

"Depression is only desire deprived
Once more unto the breach and fuck my getting it right
We've died for so long
Let's just get out alive"
Nerina Pallot – "Damascus"

Looking to the future

Anger and internal emotion can be a great energy that can be constructive to us, not as often seen by services as just destructive, (for example assertiveness and questioning your treatment may be interpreted as aggressive) but rather as a force which motivates by harnessing our emotions and can lead us to change and resolution. It is a sad fact that with psychic distress comes a narrower vision of the world, as in effect our world shrinks. There are many losses – loss of confidence, friendships, for some maybe the loss of their job, university placement, finances, security, home and perhaps most poignant, the loss of dreams. It can feel that the future you dreamt of has been snatched from you and life will never be the same again. Goffman described this process as stripping, where the layers of a person are systematically stripped from them by supposedly helping systems until all that one has left is a small core which can erode. Building our resilience helps us to re-apply these layers.

We know from personal experience that anger and bitterness can colour our vision once the bright future we hoped for starts to fall apart. Even knowing that others have reclaimed their lives doesn't inspire once you feel this low, and even skills and things you used to enjoy hold little interest any more.

There are no easy answers at this stage – the key is to treat yourself kindly, remember this is temporary and believe it or not, things really can get better for you. However a certain degree of commitment and personal responsibility is required in order to reclaim your future.

Often it is when we become stuck in the past and haven't made sense of certain situations and events that prevents us from embracing a different future. Some of the exercises we have included in this book are there to help you explore such situations and may raise some difficult memories for you. Try to ensure you are able to talk things over with someone you trust and who cares about you.

Instead of thinking of the future as something large and threatening and in terms of years ahead, learn to concentrate on getting through one day, today as best you can. Think of this as a new beginning.

"Today's burden can be endured.
It is when tomorrow's burdens are added to the burdens of today
That the weight is more than one can bear"

Timelines

It may prove useful to draw up a timeline for yourself. Biographical Timeline Planning developed by Dr. Beth Barol is an evolving process based in part on the work of Herb Lovett, William Bento, and Robert Post.

It is a facilitated process that looks at life events and interventions. This tool is especially valuable if people are finding it challenging to support you and you want to develop a team that has a better understanding of how your life has influenced who you are today so that appropriate supports will be developed.

A biographical timeline can be used as a preparation to other person centered planning processes. Timelines are often a valuable aid in showing you where and when significant events have taken place in your life, and may be an indicator of how these events still influence your life or act as a trigger. From birth to now, you may wish to include:

- Family events and celebrations
- Schooling and your experiences of education
- Occupations, courses, and jobs you have done
- Admissions to hospital
- Times of distress and the situations causing this
- Bereavements and your thoughts and feelings about these events
- Positives in your life, when it was going really well and good things that happened. By knowing the good as well we can understand ourselves.

Constructing a timeline

Fill in the major events in your life, marking the year (and month if possible) with positive experiences above the line, negative experiences below the line. This is an important visual reminder that positive happy events are always deserving of a higher place in our consciousness. Sometimes the events are interlinked, e.g. an example of a negative event may be the death of a loved one – a positive example might be a particularly happy Christmas or holiday with that person.

Past   **Positive events**   **present**

Negative events

Personal Narratives – telling your story

Telling your story in your own words and from your own perspective can prove helpful on many levels. There are many ways in which you can use your story, indeed telling your story in itself is described by many, as helpful.

One way of approaching this is to construct a personal narrative – the story of your experiences. This could be in a written form, with accompanying pictures, doodles, poetry etc. or as a recorded journey of your life.

Life stories are important for identity as they tell us who we are. They help to confirm sameness rather than accentuating difference – trauma / emotional distress is a common denominator. You may discover new insights into your personal experiences and seeing (or hearing) the story may enable you to make sense of your life. Most importantly it is a totally unique perspective – your insider view.

If you find writing your story frightening, or you don't want others to know the story there are things that you can do. Write it as a novel, change names and places, keep it safe and never let others see it. When complete you can burn or bury it, if it helps you move on. A friend of ours even had a burial ceremony to say goodbye to the old her, the self of difficult experiences.

There may be some difficulties – it may involve re-living challenging memories and it can prove a time consuming process (especially the write-up) but here are some ideas of how to frame your story. Take as long as you need to write up your story.

My Story
What I remember about my home(s) :
When I was a young child I:
When I was a teenager I:
What I remember about school is:
The friends I remember:
As I grow older I:
The people and places I remember are:
The important events in my life have been, (good, bad):
In the past, I have seen various professionals and services including:
The way in which services and professionals describe me is:
The way I would describe myself is;
These service-providers suggested that I would achieve the following:
What I wish to achieve is;
The things which I choose to continue talking about include:
In the past I liked:
In the past I did not like:
My feelings about the past are:
As a result of my previous experiences, the future should involve:

Talk the above over with someone you trust

Sometimes we can't find the words to express how we feel. Don't worry – you may communicate in different ways – music, for example or art. Compilation CDs of music tracks which "speak" to you, describe how you are feeling, make you think of experiences you've been through or emotions you can't put a name to can be a powerful tool for helping with psychic distress.

Colour Diaries

Colour, shape and design may enable us to express deep emotions and tap into a deeper level of understanding. Doodling or drawing using a range of colours can release emotions that we are unable to express in other ways. Using colour as an expression enables you to have your own, secret language which releases your innermost feelings based on instinct of shape, depth and intensity of the colours you use. You may wish to give the colours you use meanings – black may represent depression, for example, and red anger, whereas green may represent hope, yellow love or happiness. Many people have discovered that they are competent, even accomplished artists, and the freedom of being able to express one's emotions in such a deeply personal way can help work through issues in a way that sometimes words can't.

Portfolios

You might prefer to keep a scrapbook of your achievements, compiling a portfolio of you as the key person, your likes, dislikes etc. Just like a scrapbook it can include articles cut from newspapers or magazines, drawings, poems, written articles or just random thoughts, observations and comments. Some of the areas to explore and develop in compiling a portfolio might be;

Relationships – self, friends, workers, colleagues, neighbours, peers, pets

Communication, language & style, verbal & non-verbal systems of communication

Rights & choices   Trust   Dislikes & Preferences

Decision-making   *Dreams & Aspirations*   *Advocacy*

Understanding the world   Holidays & Travel

Occupation   Leisure, Sport & Relaxation

Interests   Culture – class, roots and family history   Spiritual Interests

Links to education services   Education & learning experiences

Lifestyle   Intentions & goals   Ways of dealing with stress

HOUSING / HOME LIFE, ENVIRONMENTAL FACTORS

Wish lists

Sometimes when we become mentally distressed our dreams for a fulfilling future seem pointless, like false hopes. But for many people just having the dream, whether or not we attain it, gives a focus to the future. Most people's dreams <u>are</u> realistic and achievable, even if it's only the essence or sense of it. We might not all get to sit on the tropical beaches of the Indian ocean but a trip to the English coast with friends can bring just as much pleasure.

Dreams don't necessarily just happen to come true, though. They do require some work and the previous example could be a lengthy process – planning where to go, who can I approach to go with me? Can I afford it, how long do I need to save for it?   Working toward your dreams is a tool for motivation, they are your desires and hopes and it is inherently positive because one doesn't have to achieve your dreams to be fulfilled, just be taking steps toward them is enough for most of us.

My dreams for the future

What are your dreams? What do you need to do to work towards the dream?

1. I would love to…

"If you don't see the gifts in a person, you are the wrong person looking"

Judith Snow

The more we dream about personal and social change,
The more we need people around us
To sustain the dream
And support us during times of struggle and disappointment.
The more people around us,
The greater the dream and
The greater our sense of hope,
The more we can change the world".

Beth Mount, 'Imperfect Change' 1990

Whatever you can do or dream…
Begin it.
Boldness has the power and magic in it
Goethe

You see things and say "Why?"
But I dream things that never were and say "Why not?"
G.B. Shaw

Had I the heavens' embroidered cloths,
Enwrought with golden and silver light,
The blue and the dim and the dark cloths
Of night and light and the half-light,
I would spread the cloths under your feet:
But I, being poor, have only my dreams;
I have spread my dreams under your feet;
Tread softly because you tread on my dreams.
"The cloths of heaven" - WB Yeats

What is your dream? What have you always wished for?
Having a dream enables us to feel optimistic about a better future, and as the song says, "You've got to have a dream, 'cos if you don't have a dream, how are you going to make a dream come true!"
If you are experiencing psychic distress it may be a vital part of your recovery for someone who cares about you to take on those feelings of optimism temporarily for you. They can encourage you to look to the future, feel positive that change will be for the better and support you to accept that life can improve.

23

Holders of hope
In her booklet, "Challenging Mental Impotence", Helen Glover, Australian Recovery Consultant, likens people on a journey through the mental health system to a railway journey where some of the stops might be Hopeless station, Sickness Station, Surrender Station (where people have given in and the system has beaten us down) and often we go round and round the circuit.

"There are" she says "windows of opportunity that we miss so many times going round. Windows of opportunity allow us to get to the other platforms on the line of our journey where there are "Holders of Hope" waiting to assist us to change journeys."

This allows access to an alternative route, via Hopeful Platforms to Fighter Station and Recovery Station. Hopefulness emerges from within, having a hint of a dream, a potential purpose and holding on to them. Many things can instil or nurture hope.

Write down when you are feeling more hopeful those things that nurture your hope.
It may be religion or spirituality, other people, meaning in suffering – these are some of the things that may sustain and encourage us.

Finding hope
If you feel you have little hope for the future, someone else could encourage you and hold that hope for you. They can do this by encouraging you, being optimistic for you and reminding you of positive things in your life. Eventually as you believe more in yourself and regain your confidence you will get your optimism back.

Who do you trust to be your Holder of hope?
Why? What is it about them that you trust?

My supporter(s) / holders of hope are…
They help me by…

It is important that your supporters know when to hold hope for you – by encouraging, being positive, having expectations of success for you, but also that they enable you to take on the role as your own holder of hope as soon as you are able and ready to!
I can help myself by…

Your experiences of "helping" services
It may be useful as part of your journey to write down your personal experiences of "helping services". Sometimes it gives a new perspective and you can start to look at things more objectively. It can also determine what has been helpful or unhelpful so you know what you need in the future.

The following may help you to construct a narrative;

My experiences of "helping" services
1. When was your first encounter with "helping" services?
2. What led up to this?
3. What do you consider the problems were?
4. What did others see the problems as being?
5. What support did you have from professionals?
6. Which workers helped? How?
7. What didn't help?
8. What treatments were you offered? How satisfied were you with this?
9. What did you expect to happen that didn't?
10. What has happened since that first encounter?
11. How long have you been receiving services?
12. What would you like to happen now?

Getting unstuck

It can be easy to feel "stuck in a moment" and it can take an enormous effort to feel positive that things will ever be any different. It can be disheartening if you do make changes but don't see the immediate results, causing you to retreat to the "stuck" place yet again.

"Don't say that later will be better
Now you're stuck in a moment
and you can't get out of it"   *U2 "Stuck in a moment"*

Something that may prove useful is to stop "beating yourself up", (this reinforces negativity and prevents you from moving forward) and to consider whether there are very good reasons why you feel the way you do. It may be that your emotional system has gone into "shutdown" mode because of overload and you need time out to re-energize. Perhaps other people have been excessively demanding of your time and attention or you have been working / studying too hard.

Maybe past or present events have totally overwhelmed you and your feelings are out of control, maybe negativity from others has rubbed off on you or possibly you are confused as to what you think or feel at all. Take a few moments to consider why you feel stuck. Once you identify some of the reasons why, and accept that "shutting down" or "shutting off" are natural responses, then it becomes easier to see that this is temporary.

Finding patterns

Patterns in life are good for maintaining positive mental health, as long as we are not too obsessive about it. If we have no structure to the day, it can prove interminably long and boring. With time on our hands it is easy to venture into mood dependent memory where if you are down at a particular time, you think of bad things that have happened to you generally at other times. This then becomes a self fulfilling prophecy of doom – bad things always happen to me!

Look for the patterns in your days
Write down for one week all the things you do from morning to night.
What do you mostly do?
Does this make you happy? If yes, great, if not, why not?

Keeping a diary

Keeping a diary is an enjoyable, inspiring, open-ended and flexible approach to personal development and reflection. You might not wish to write daily but rather weekly or as and when something inspires you. You do not have to write huge amounts, and you may prefer to include doodles, pictures or poems instead of or as well as the written word. Diaries can prove useful and effective in identifying patterns in your life and showing where change can occur.

Warning signs

There are a number of warning signs that inform all of us when we are becoming stressed or unwell. Typically, many people choose to ignore the signs hoping things will improve, but if left over a long period, the following can escalate to an unmanageable level

- Not sleeping
- Not eating
- Staying away from people
- Drinking more alcohol than usual
- Using recreational drugs (more than usual)
- Irritability
- Forgetfulness
- Lack of concentration

What are your warning signs that things are deteriorating?

By knowing and recognising your signs it may be possible to plan for and thus avoid crisis.

A useful way of doing this might be to write out how things are when you are feeling well so you have a guideline of what is normal for you. It will also help other people to recognise when you veer away from your usual patterns.

Is your usual demeanour loud? Quiet?
How do you usually interact with people? Are you talkative? Are you sometimes withdrawn or shy?
Are there any colloquialisms you use? Do you usually swear?

Profile of me on a good day
I am …. (List all of the things people could expect of you when you feel o.k.)

If I show the following signs, it may indicate I am stressed / not feeling well……..
List things that would be unusual for you to do, say, express, behave etc

By prearranging roles and jobs for other people to take on should you feel unable to cope, you are assured that the essentials are covered and will worry less.

Make a list of your friends and family and identify the action(s) you would wish them to take.
This might include contacting a loved one, other telephone calls, arranging childcare, sorting out my mail / bills / food / feeding animals / watering plants etc. until I feel able to cope. Long and short term planning may need to be considered.

You can draw this up as an Advance Directive and ensure your friends; family, workers and colleagues know and agree to your requests. If you do not have family nearby and find yourself alone and isolated, there are organisations and support networks who may be able to help. Often local churches have pastoral visitors; there may be buddying schemes in your locality. Consider joining a singles club or speed dating!

Identifying the real problems

By critically appraising what you feel the real problems are, then you have something to work with. Often we make the mistake of seeing the end result as the problem, as with depression. It's not depression that is the problem, it's the way the depression affects your life or others around you. Once you accept that and start to examine those areas you begin to have more control over the experience.

Think of your problem area. Often we think that the technical things we are told, diagnosis, symptoms etc are the problem when in fact the problems are often just consequences of those things like not sleeping, not trusting, feeling guilty and shameful, self blame, upsetting others

What is the context it arises within; does it relate to your life experiences and timelines?
What is your understanding of it?
How does it cause disruption in your life?
What distress does it cause you?
What distress does it cause others?
How do you try to cope and survive?

Focussing techniques

Mental focussing involves directing your thoughts towards a positive outcome. In order to clear your mind so that you are able to do this, try this simple exercise –
Part one
1. Get a pen and paper ready to write down your thoughts
2. Sit in a comfortable chair, take a few deep breaths and relax
3. Now write down all of the words that come into your mind, it doesn't matter whether they make sense or not! No one else need see this.
4. Let the words flow effortlessly and fluently for five minutes or so

Now take several deep breaths, read your words back if you wish, it's not important. What is important is that the jumble of thoughts that was in your head has now transferred to the page and can be destroyed, leaving you with a calmer, serene mind which can now focus on your chosen positive outcome. Decide what that outcome is to be. What would you love to achieve?
Part two
1. Close your eyes for ten minutes, relax and take two deep breaths
2. Believe that you can achieve this thing
3. Think how it feels to achieve it
4. Who else is involved?
5. What words describe the achievement?

Write down as much as you can remember thinking during the ten minutes. Keep that piece of paper somewhere that you can look at it to remind you of the positivity you felt. It doesn't matter whether that achievement comes to fruition or not, the important thing is that sensing of the possibility of it happening.

Another way to get in touch with your creativity is to pay attention to your dreams. You don't need any specialised knowledge. Just write down your dreams each morning – using the present tense to do this can help take you back to the dream scenario – taking note of any words or phrases which particularly "speak" to you. These can be triggers for an especially imaginative piece of work. American writer Joyce Carol Oates has said that her novel "Bellefleur" was inspired by a dream of a walled garden which haunted her for years until she felt she had to write about it.

Art / Music as therapy

Using any of the art forms as a creative expression of how you are feeling can be very therapeutic. Drawing, painting, collage, photography, sculpture, modelling, needlework, etc. can be an excellent way of tapping into and releasing our deeper emotions.

If you feel angry, bitter, frustrated or despondent depict it visually. Keeping your work and later looking at it in chronological order can also be a significant indicator of the range of emotions experienced and how far you have moved on. If you are not particularly artistic, consider making compilation CDs or tapes which allow you a range of emotions – anger, hurt, frustration, hope, fear, love. Enjoy the experience of "going into" the music wholeheartedly and let the emotions take over temporarily, but bring yourself back to a "grounded" space by playing something calming at the end.

Knowing self

There are varying aspects of self and knowledge of each aspect helps the journey to recovery.
- Self Awareness – knowledge of what makes us tick
- Self Esteem- a good opinion of ourself, happy with who we are
- Self Confidence- confident in our behaviour, our actions etc.
- Self Determination – ability to make decisions for ourselves without outside influence
- Self Discipline – the ability to discipline our own feelings, desires etc.
- Self Expression – the ability to express our personality, feelings etc. as in painting, poetry
- Self Possession- having control of one's emotions
- Self Realisation – the fulfilment of our potential or abilities
- Self Respect – a proper sense of our own dignity and integrity

Which of these comments would you apply to yourself at the moment?

I want to destroy myself
I hate myself
I dislike myself lots
I don't like myself, sometimes
I have my strengths and weaknesses
I'm OK, mostly
I'm really good
I am fantastic
I'm God's gift to the planet!

Why do you feel this way?
Here are some questions that may help you identify your good points.

1. What do you like about yourself, however small and fleeting?
2. What positive qualities do you possess?
3. What have you achieved in your life however small?
4. What challenges have you faced?
5. What gifts or talents do you have however modest?
6. What skills have you acquired?
7. What do others like or value in you?
8. What qualities that you value in others do you share?
9. What aspects of yourself would you appreciate if they were aspects of another person?
10. What small positives are you discounting?
11. What are the bad things you are not?
12. How might someone who cares about you describe you?

If possible, talk this over with someone you trust and who cares about you (an ally). Do they agree with your answers? Repeat this exercise on different days. Are there certain times when you feel like this? Is it fairly constant? What changes would you wish to make if you could? Which are possible?

What is healthy self-esteem?
The following factors could describe someone with healthy self esteem.
- Confident, but not arrogant or over-bearing
- Feels loved by others and accepts self
- Not devastated by criticism
- Not overly defensive
- Very self-aware i.e. knows strengths and weaknesses
- Doesn't put others down
- Not driven to prove oneself
- Clear at communicating needs
- Able to laugh at self and at life
- Good coping skills
- Fairly contented
- Optimistic, even excited by the future

Increasing your self esteem involves self encouragement and activity. Sitting around and waiting to feel better about yourself will most likely lead to failure. Take action of any sort and you will almost certainly feel better about yourself

What builds self worth?
- Being accepted and supported
- Embarking on a journey of self-discovery
- Encouraging self-disclosure
- Re-examining goals and priorities
- Learning coping skills
- Avoiding destructive influences
- Knowing how to assert oneself
- Pampering oneself without feeling guilty
- Learning to give to others

Ways of building esteem
- **Maintain good health**
- **Try to live a balanced life-style**
- **Understand yourself accurately and honestly**
- **Learn from mistakes and try not to repeat**
- **Forgive yourself when you make a mistake**
- **Set achievable targets and goals**
- **Change the way you speak to yourself**
- **Don't beat yourself up**
- **Celebrate your achievements**
- **Receive counselling to deal with issues from the past**
- **Go on an assertiveness course**

Now thats what i call BRAVE

Knowing others

It is a sad reality that often when you become mentally unwell friends and colleagues drop out of your life. This may happen for a number of reasons – sometimes they are unable to deal with their own emotional distress of seeing you unwell. Sometimes people's lives are busy and you just get overlooked. It is not necessarily malicious, though it can be hurtful. What you find, however, is that the people who do stick with you are your genuine friends and will always support you.

There is a vast difference between being lonely and being alone. Some people enjoy their own company. Others prefer to have companionship much of the time, and sometimes when our sense of self is not as developed as it could be we can cling to relationships, however abusive, rather than face being on our own. This results sometimes in people exploiting and manipulating us into situations we are not comfortable with. This is difficult then to address and leads to renewed lack of esteem and confidence; you're back on a downward spiral.

Questions to ask yourself
1. **Is this a helpful or unhelpful relationship?**
2. **Are others "taking" from you constantly without giving in return?**
3. **Are you supporting other people financially?**
4. **Are you always supporting others emotionally?**
5. **Does the person make you feel good about yourself?**
6. **Do they put you down?**

Discuss the above with someone you trust who cares about you

Understanding your triggers

There may be events or circumstances that crop up which cause you to not only remember painful things in the past, but to feel catapulted back there. This can be particularly frustrating as you try to move on with life as it feels that you will always be caught up in a negative spiral by things beyond your control. It is possible, however to recognise and deal with many of the trigger factors, and in some cases anticipate and either deal with them or avoid them.

"Known" triggers

Some trigger factors are identifiable as such, and ways of coping can be built into your personal planning. Examples of "known" triggers may include;

- Anniversaries or dates of significant events – loss, bereavement, accidents, trauma
- Times of year – Christmas, change of clocks,
- Life events-relationship breakdown, loss of a person/pet/support/identity/job etc. Bullying and intimidation
- Stress generally, feeling mad or like you are losing control
- Overwhelm—feeling overwhelmed by certain events or the snowball of disaster, normally people can feel resilient but it is the combination of factors that causes overwhelm
- Change or new experiences- Living alone for first time, a new theology or religion, beginning a course of study, childbirth
- Days of the week – weekends can be a period of triggers if you spend them alone
- Places – that remind you of the past in a non helpful way
- Others attitudes – sarcasm, indifference, bullying attitudes, hostility, belittling may trigger memories of other people who treated you this way in the past

"Unknown" triggers

More difficult to anticipate and plan for are the more subtle triggers which you may or may not be consciously aware of and can crop up taking you unawares. These are things which act on one or more of our senses and flood our minds with memories. Often it is as a response to these triggers that "flashbacks" are experienced. As you learn to understand yourself better and become more aware of your triggers it will give you more control in your life and lessen the impact of these negative experiences. Examples of "unknown" triggers may include;

- A certain piece of music
- Certain smells
- Certain tastes
- Touch – fabrics, textures etc.
- Certain household objects
- Certain sounds
- Weather
- Faces or body shapes that remind you of someone else

The following exercise may help you to identify some of your triggers

Times of the year
Write down your positive and negative experiences relating to specific months of the year to gain an overview of how the year's anniversaries are significant. You might wish to include births, deaths, hospital admissions, traumatic events, significant loss or change, etc.

	Positive events	**Negative events**
January		
February		
March		
April		
May		
June		
July		
August		
September		
October		
November		
December		

Is there a pattern to the year? Are some months laden with events? If so, it may be that this becomes a difficult period of time for you as there are so many memories attached to that particular time. With awareness that this is the case you can prepare for those difficult times. It may be that you need more help and support from other people around these times.
If possible, discuss this with someone you trust and who cares about you.

Chapter 5
The THRIVE© Approach
Healing

"And we'll walk down the avenue and we'll smile
And we'll say baby ain't it all worthwhile when the healing has begun"
"And the healing has begun" - Van Morrison

Who can say when healing truly begins? Often it is only with the wisdom of hindsight that we recognise important milestones and turning points in life. But there are key features that we can nurture and develop to get us started. It is well documented that having some degree of hope for oneself is vital to recovery but there may be times when all hope is lost and then it's important that others hold on to hope for you until you feel well enough to continue being hopeful for yourself. Optimism can influence and be a starting point for constructive change so learning to maintain a hopeful outlook is a way of embarking upon the healing process.

If there are core problems then they can be healed, it requires that you know what needs healing and find a way to heal. There is an old saying, "It's not the problem that is the problem, but how you deal with the problem that's the problem" This is often true for people who have accepted psychiatry's view of their illness and then it becomes the stumbling block. For example, self injury and voices may often be regarded as the problem and medication usually prescribed as an answer. Rather than seeing these coping strategies as the problem, if we understand them to be the messenger of an altogether different problem such as abuse or bullying we have something to work with – something to heal. Medication may or may not be important in this context.

Allowing oneself to heal is another milestone. For many reasons – guilt, shame, self loathing, disgust, lack of self belief, worthlessness etc. people block their own healing. Taking a conscious decision to say, "Sod it, I'm worth it!" and deliberately treating oneself well is paramount to healing. Sometimes people assume this is selfish – the paradigm is that you can't love others until you love yourself; therefore it is not selfish but a necessity.

Healing may be a difficult thing to face up to if your experiences in the past were of violence, sexual or psychological abuse or bullying, as it may (though not necessarily) bring things up for you that you'd "put away". A friend of ours, talking about his experience of receiving counselling for childhood sexual abuse speaks of how "I knew I had to let the lid off the "box in the corner". It was painful, taking it off, sorting everything out and discovering what was deep inside. But I'm glad I did it. It feels as though I've rearranged it and made sense of it all".

Other people have said that their childhood experiences are distant memories which they have sifted through but have no desire to go back to. Like putting the box in storage and throwing away the key!

Only you know which approach is right for you.

"I hurt myself today to see if I still feel
I focus on the pain the only thing that's real
The needle tears a hole, the old familiar sting
Try to kill it all away but I remember everything
"Hurt" – Trent Reznor (9 inch nails)

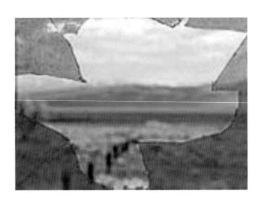

Finding yourself not guilty

Self blame is often a major problem for adults who experience various traumas in childhood and early adolescence. This is most easily seen in the area of childhood sexual abuse where the majority of survivors of such experiences feel responsible both for the abuse and even for the person who abused them. It is important to separate here the rational from the emotional self.

If you were abused as a child you can intellectually and rationally conclude that it was not your fault, you were young, vulnerable, alone, exploited. Emotionally however you still feel responsible. Much of this is because of the way you were groomed to be abused. One of the stages of grooming for abuse is to prevent the young person from disclosing the abuse - what better way than encouraging the child to take responsibility so that they feel it is within their control to stop what is happening and to say no, then as an adult no matter how much they rationalize they will still feel guilty. Recognition of the tactics of people who abuse children and their purpose can be a first stage in healing the hurt and finding yourself not guilty, emotionally as well as rationally.

Many adults who were abused as children may find it difficult to talk about their childhood; workers may find it difficult to hear. Yet statistically, many of the people who end up in mental health services have faced some sort of abuse. (Amongst adolescents in psychiatric services who reported abuse 83% cut themselves) Some would say that the system further abuses them by labelling, medicating and institutionalising rather than dealing with the original problem

It may be that you feel that you missed out on childhood completely; or you feel "stuck" as that frightened child at times.

"I sometimes feel like a little girl, like when I was being abused.
I never had a childhood, not a proper one"
Vanessa

Do you consider yourself to have been abused when you were a child? Sexual abuse can take many different forms, and cover a wide range of unwanted behaviours, including
- Unwanted contact
- Treating person as sex object
- Forcing pornography on victim
- Hounding for sex
- Forced penetration – vaginal, anal, oral
- Forced penetration using hand or implement
- Forcing partner into acts and rituals they dislike
- Rape
- Made to masturbate self
- Made to masturbate abuser
- Made to have sex with other children
- Taking photos and misusing them
- Fondling children inappropriately
- Made to kiss abuser

If you consider that you were abused, is it a major issue for you, do you feel responsible, do you feel worthless, and are you ashamed? This is precisely how abusers work and "groom" their targets to ensure cooperation and secrecy, and it is a very insidious process which leaves adult survivors of childhood sexual abuse still experiencing those emotions. There is overwhelming evidence in the research literature that a significant proportion of adults who experienced the trauma of childhood abuse will experience social, emotional and psychological problems of a serious and disruptive nature in their adult life
Problems may include:

- Physical injuries
- Fear
- Depression
- Self-destructive behaviours
- Low self esteem
- Feelings of confusion
- Sexual acting out behaviours
- Nightmares
- Hostility
- Phobias
- Antisocial behaviour
- Socialization problems

A way of reclaiming power is to find yourself "innocent" and "forgive" yourself.

Practical ways of reclaiming power;
- Visual props. Compare a child's shoe to that of an adult – how realistically can that child be to blame for anything?
- Write a letter to the abuser then burn it – symbolically letting go,
- Draw / paint pictures which represent the situation

Healing the hurt
Physical scars / psychological scars

Physical scars are the ones people can see and empathise with. Psychological scars may be much more painful to bear. No one can tell for sure by looking at another person whether they have been subjected to abuse, and all too often that abuse has been kept hidden. This can keep the wounds raw.

"It may be a long and winding road to recovery. Those supporting need lots of patience. Victims need to know that there may be scars!"   *Chris Rankin*

There are many different forms of abuse --emotional, psychological, prejudicial, verbal, sexual abuse to name but a few. To abuse is to misuse power, authority, position, privilege, trust or strength in order to mistreat another human being. Sometimes this is unintentional, but often it is deliberate. It may involve the most disturbing inflictions that can lead to physical, emotional, mental, social, financial or spiritual damage. If you have suffered any form of abuse you may experience some or all of the following feelings;

Guilt	Feeling dirty
Unhappiness	Naughty
Shame	Disloyal
Fear	Special
Self blame	Different

If you find that you are experiencing any of the above it may prove useful to discuss with someone you trust and who cares about you.

Precious and fragile things
Need special handling
My God what have we done to You?

We always try to share
The tenderest of care
Now look what we have put You through...

Things get damaged
Things get broken
I thought we'd manage
But words left unspoken
Left us so brittle
There was so little left to give

Angels with silver wings
Shouldn't know suffering
I wish I could take the pain for You

If God has a master plan
That only He understands
I hope it's Your eyes He's seeing through

Depeche Mode "Precious"

Valuing self
- Have some time regularly where you do exactly what YOU want to do
- Take some time to be completely alone and enjoy your own company
- Aim to achieve something each day; just a walk to the shops or writing a poem can make you feel good about yourself
- Prioritise things, especially the boring things like paying bills, and then reward yourself with a small treat when you've done them all
- Remind yourself of skills / gifts you have – everyone is good at something!
- Plan a special meal for yourself, or invite a friend to share it.

"TREAT YOURSELF AS YOUR OWN BEST FRIEND"

Don't rely on others for your happiness / self worth. When we rely on others approval of us, we are placing all of our value in someone else's hands. This means our self confidence is totally dependent on how other people feel or act toward us.

It also means we are defined by others views, and in the mental health system it is easy to fall into the trap of seeing ourselves as others see us.

But others opinions are not necessarily the truth. Many people have been informed they have "an enduring mental illness" and told "This is as good as it gets" or "you will need to take medication the rest of your life". Allowing someone else to define your life is not compulsory! This is what children do out of necessity, because they don't have the inner resources as we do as adults. But as adults, we can begin to learn how to give ourselves confident feelings and to maintain them.

Being aware of what a vulnerable thing it is to put our whole self worth into someone else's hand, might help to avoid this pitfall. Maintaining our self worth or self confidence might also require reminding ourselves of the things that we value in ourselves, keeping in mind those qualities we really appreciate.

Another way to rebuild our self confidence is to try doing and risking things that we've never tried before. There's always a little bit of a challenge in doing new things and just the act of accepting these challenges, some little and some big, whether we are successful or not, often increases our self confidence.

However, when our sense of self is diminished it can not only prevent us taking the risks of new experiences, but limits our everyday activities. It can be excruciatingly painful to even get out of bed and through the front door! The healing process is about recognising this, and building up with small steps. One of the ways we work with people is to ask them to draw up a wish list, and then support the steps to achieving the wish.

My wish list
Make a list of all the things you would wish to participate in or achieve over the next two years, (these can be anything at all e.g. getting a bus into town, joining a college course, going to the seaside, having a massage etc.)

Don't give a time limit to any of these, but look at your list and see what are in reality the most achievable.

Now, imagine it has actually been done.

Write down next to the event how you feel and what was good about it. Then make a list next to the event of what you would need to do to achieve it, breaking things down into small, manageable steps, e.g.

Having a massage	Feel refreshed, calm & energised	Need to save £? each week
		Can I afford it?
		Get costings
		Phone to see where I can go
		Is there a cheaper option?
		Maybe a local college does it?
		Think how I get there
		Am I able to go alone?
		Would someone else go with me?
		When would be a good time to go?

It is important that as you fulfil each wish you tick it off. You may be surprised how easy it is once you get into this way of thinking how the confidence from achieving one thing leads to the others being achieved. Don't see the main aim as just getting to the end of the list – it's more important that you enjoy each achievement - and don't "beat yourself up" if progress seems slow. If this is the case check that you are including realistic, achievable goals as well as the more optimistic ones. It's not completing the list that is important it's the resolve to address the list.

Treatments and therapies

The following therapies, complimentary therapies and alternatives may prove useful in your recovery. Courses and treatments vary in cost and duration and some are more widely available than others. However, even if you are not able to access these particular therapies, it may be of immense help to inform yourself about them either by reading or accessing information on the internet.

The Human Givens Approach

The Human Givens Approach works on a very simple and straightforward principle. As human beings we come into this world with basic physical needs such as the need for shelter, warmth and safety, and with emotional needs, such as the need for love, security, connection and control, and the self-esteem which arises from feeling competent in different areas of our lives. We also have the innate resources to help us meet these needs, including: memory, imagination, problem solving abilities, self-awareness and a range of complementary thinking styles to employ in various different situations. It is these needs and resources together, which are built into our biology that make up the Human Givens. Our emotional needs include:

- Security — safe territory and an environment which allows us to develop fully
- Attention (to give and receive it) — a form of nutrition
- Sense of autonomy and control — having volition to make responsible choices
- Being emotionally connected to others
- Feeling part of a wider community
- Friendship, intimacy — to know that at least one other person accepts us totally as we are
- Privacy — opportunity to reflect and consolidate experience
- Sense of status within social groupings
- Sense of competence and achievement
- Meaning and purpose — which come from being stretched in what we do and think.

Along with physical and emotional needs nature gave us guidance systems to help us meet them. We call these 'resources'. The resources nature gave us to help us meet our needs include:

- The ability to develop complex long term memory, which enables us to add to our innate knowledge and learn
- The ability to build rapport, empathise and connect with others
- Imagination, which enables us to focus our attention away from our emotions, use language and problem solve more creatively and objectively
- A conscious, rational mind that can check out emotions, question, analyse and plan
- The ability to 'know' — that is, understand the world unconsciously through metaphorical pattern matching
- An observing self — that part of us that can step back, be more objective and be aware of itself as a unique centre of awareness, apart from intellect, emotion and conditioning

Neuro-Linguistic Programming (NLP)

Although NLP is probably most popularly known for its applications within therapy, it is not a therapy in itself but rather the study of communication and cognitive processes, and how these create and affect our behaviour. NLP is built on the understanding that our experience of the world is processed through our own individual filters (including our memories, decisions, values and beliefs, etc) which code, order and give meaning to our experiences, and create our perceptions of ourselves and the world. We each have personal 'programming' of which we are largely unaware, including strategies and repeated patterns of thinking that affect our emotions, physiology and behaviour.

At the heart of NLP lies the modelling process where techniques are used to discover a person's strategies and thinking patterns. By adopting these patterns, it becomes possible to replicate that person's behaviour and results in order to, for example, learn how that person does something particularly well. This use of NLP to 'model excellence' is why it is increasingly encountered in many fields outside of therapy, including teaching, business and sports performance.

NLP's therapeutic roots lie in the mid 1970's when its creators modelled well-known therapists who constantly achieved excellent results with their clients. This work began what is a constantly growing and developing body of knowledge and the approach and techniques which grew from it form the basis of what is commonly thought of as NLP in the therapeutic setting today. NLP differs from other 'talking therapies' by emphasising communication with the client's unconscious mind with the intention of interrupting programs that result in unwanted negative thoughts and/or behaviour, and installing new programs to assist the client in creating new possibilities and positive outcomes.

NLP is known for its ability to facilitate change in an individual far quicker than many conventional counselling-type therapies and, whilst it is possibly most well-known for providing incredibly rapid relief from the symptoms of unwanted emotional and behavioural responses (phobias, anxiety, etc), it is also used successfully with physical symptoms and illness. Some practitioners use NLP alone and others use it alongside other therapies and techniques including hypnosis, coaching, Emotional Freedom Technique (EFT) and Time Line Therapy™ (TLT). There are various levels of qualification in NLP and, as with all therapies it is recommended that you find an experienced practitioner with previous experience relevant to your area of interest.
Stephen Swayn - (Developing Possibilities"

Time Line Therapy™ (TLT)

Developed by Dr Tad James in the 1980s, TLT is based on the belief that our unconscious mind stores and organises all of memories in our own individual Time Line. Practitioners use light trance techniques and communication with the client's unconscious mind to guide clients along their Time Line and release unwanted negative emotions including anger, sadness, fear, hurt and guilt, and limiting decisions and beliefs. Negative emotions are released back at the first event or root cause and on all subsequent events where that emotion is present, enabling the client to have emotional freedom and balance around experiences which previously caused distress. Any positive learnings which arose from these experiences are preserved and clients often report receiving new and positive learnings and insights from the process.

Practitioners can also work with clients to support them in achieving future goals or desired outcomes. A major advantage of TLT in comparison with counselling therapies is that it does not require 'talking through' or re-experiencing negative memories or events and is therefore an emotionally-easier process for the client. Most significantly, these techniques are used successfully with many varied issues, including physical symptoms and illness, and enable clients to make long-lasting changes in a very rapid way.

Readers should note that there are several unconnected therapies that use similar terminology (timeline, time release, walking the timeline). Practitioners of TLT as detailed here must first be qualified in NLP and will have a NLP qualification level to correspond to the level at which they practise TLT. Time Line Therapy™ as detailed here always appears as a trademarked name and practitioners will be members of the Time Line Therapy™ Association.
Steven Swayn - Developing Possibilities

Cognitive Behavioural Therapy (CBT)

CBT is a combination of cognitive therapy, which examines unwanted thoughts, attitudes, and beliefs (called cognitive processes) and behavioural therapy, which focuses on behaviour in response to those thoughts. CBT is based on the belief that most unhealthy modes of thinking and behaving have been learned over a long period of time. Using a set of structured techniques, a CBT therapist aims to identify thinking that causes problematic feelings and behaviour. The client then learns to change this thinking which, in turn, leads to more appropriate and positive responses.

For example, negative thoughts usually lead to upsetting or angry feelings which then affect our mood and our behaviour. If a person is unable to counter such thoughts with a more positive stance, a negative spiral ensues and perceptions of a situation can become distorted. CBT encourages the person to challenge their beliefs about themselves and their abilities so that they achieve a more realistic view of the situation.

CBT is becoming more readily available through local health services and through private practitioners as it has a well developed evidence base for its efficacy and is generally quite a short term intervention that helps people to manage their own unhelpful thoughts feelings and behaviours

Solution – focussed Brief Therapy (SBT)

Solution-focussed Brief Therapy is an approach which emphasizes *finding solutions rather than developing explanations for problems*. Solution-Focussed Brief Therapy is short-term, meaning that goals are usually accomplished in a limited number of sessions... all brief therapists have at least one thing in common—they are task-oriented. Clients are asked to set goals early on so that progress can be closely monitored at each session. How can brief therapy be so brief?

Rather than delving into past origins of the problem, brief therapists are more interested in the present and the future. By identifying each person's role in the way the problem is being handled today, brief therapists obtain the raw data necessary to generate prescriptions for change. By so doing, lengthy reviews of personal histories are bypassed.

More importantly though, SBT therapists focus on the future, helping people to envision what their lives will be like without the problems. Unlike psychodynamic or psychoanalytic approaches which emphasize how problems develop, SBT asks: "What do you want to become?" and "What are the necessary steps to get there?" Therapy becomes less explanation-oriented and more solution-oriented, a process which takes considerably less time.

The following principles sum up solution focussed brief therapy
(1) If it ain't broke, don't fix it:
(2) Once you know what works, do more of it;
(3) If it doesn't work then don't do it again, do something different.

Equine Assisted Psychotherapy

Equine Assisted Psychotherapy (EAP) is an emerging field in which horses are used as a tool for emotional growth and learning. EAP is a collaborative effort between a licensed therapist and a horse professional. Because of its intensity and effectiveness, it is considered a short-term or "brief" approach. EAP is experiential in nature. This means that participants learn about themselves and others by participating in activities with the horses, and then processing (or discussing) feelings, behaviors, and patterns.
EAP addresses a variety of mental health and human development needs including behavioral issues, attention deficit disorder, substance abuse, eating disorders, abuse issues, depression, anxiety, relationship problems and communication needs.

Aromatherapy

Aromatherapy means "treatment using scents". It is a holistic treatment of caring for the body with pleasant smelling botanical oils such as rose, lemon, lavender and peppermint. The essential oils are added to the bath or massaged into the skin, inhaled directly or diffused to scent an entire room. Aromatherapy is used for the relief of pain, care for the skin, alleviate tension and fatigue and invigorate the entire body. Essential oils can affect the mood, alleviate fatigue, reduce anxiety and promote relaxation. When inhaled, they work on the brain and nervous system through stimulation of the olfactory nerves.

The essential oils are aromatic essences extracted from plants, flowers, trees, fruits, bark, grasses and seeds with distinctive therapeutic, psychological, and physiological properties, which improve and prevent illness. There are about 150 essential oils. Most of these oils have antiseptic properties; some are antiviral, anti-inflammatory, pain-relieving, antidepressant and expectorant. Other properties of the essential oils which are taken advantage of in aromatherapy are their stimulation, relaxation, digestion improvement, and diuretic properties. To get the maximum benefit from essential oils, it should be made from natural, pure raw materials. Synthetically made oils do not work.

Reflexology

Reflexology is the application of pressure, stretch and movement to the feet and hands to effect corresponding parts of the body. Reflexologists view the feet and hands as a mirror image of the body. By applying technique a reflexologist can break up patterns of stress in other parts of the body. Pressure applied to the feet generates a signal through the peripheral nervous system. From there it enters the central nervous system where it is processed in various parts of the brain. It is then relayed to the internal organs to allocate the necessary adjustments in fuel and oxygen, Finally a response is fashioned that is sent onto the motor system.

In general terms the benefits of reflexology have to do with the reduction of stress. Because the feet and hands help set the tension level for the rest of the body they are an easy way to interrupt the stress signal and reset homeostasis, the body's equilibrium. Reflexology is a complement to standard medical care. It should not be construed as medical advice. It should not be a replacement to medical help.

Indian Head Massage

Indian Head Massage is a treatment based on old Ayurvedic techniques involving work on the upper back, shoulders, neck, scalp and face. A variety of massage movements are used to relieve accumulated tension, stimulate circulation and restore joint movement. IHM is also used to aid the condition and health of the hair, particularly when combined with the use of natural organic oils. Indian Head Massage is used by practitioners to help reduce stress and fatigue, increase mental clarity, and relax and rejuvenate the receiver. A treatment will last between 20 minutes to one hour.

Emotional Freedom Technique (EFT)

EFT (Emotional Freedom Technique) is a therapeutic approach and a self-help tool developed in the 1990s by Gary Craig, an engineer and a personal development coach, from the work of Dr Roger Callahan. EFT is a fairly simple procedure which can be learnt in a short period of time for self-help purposes. EFT combines stimulation of acupressure points with cognitive restructuring (specially worded affirmation). There is extensive anecdotal evidence for EFT providing relief from a wide variety of conditions, both physical and emotional.

EFT practitioners describe their therapy as an 'emotional form of acupuncture'. A client is assisted in tuning in to their problem; the practitioner will then use fingertips to tap a map of points, and a series of affirmations to bring about balance. The technique is said to aid many conditions from Anxiety and stress, to phobias, compulsions and pain. The technique can be self administered after a short period of study.

The most common explanation of how EFT works relies on the belief in energy system that originates within the Traditional Chinese Medicine. It is thought that the energy (known as variously in different cultures as chi, prana, life force, etc) runs through a number of meridians (channels of energy) through our body, and when we are not well, can't cope with everyday problems, over-react to situations, etc, it is said that the energy is out of balance in our body. EFT procedure is said to restore the balance within the meridian system *in relation to a specific problem or issue.*

Argentinean Dr Andrade who conducted EFT trials with thousands of anxiety patients with significant effects, proposed a neurological explanation of how EFT and related techniques could work. The tapping (or other types of pressure) of acupressure points stimulate mechanoreceptors in our skin. The acupuncture/acupressure points have a particularly high concentration of mechanoreceptors, free nerve endings, and neurovascular density. The signal that is generated when tapping eventually reaches the amygdala, hippocampus, and other structures where the emotional problem has neurological entity, and the signal apparently disrupts established patterns. One hypothesis is that the signal sent by tapping "collides" with the signal produced by thinking about the problem, introducing "noise" into the emotional process, which alters its nature and its capacity to produce symptoms. Enhanced serotonin secretion also correlates with tapping specific points

A free 79 page EFT manual can be downloaded from Gary Craig's popular website, www.emofree.com, where training videos/DVDs can also be obtained at cost price. If you buy a set of videos/DVDs, you are allowed to copy it up to 100 times as long as you give the copies away and don't sell them. There is a wealth of information on using EFT for every conceivable issue or ailment on the website which is well worth researching if you are serious about using EFT for yourself or friends and family.
Masha Bennett – Practical Happiness

Therapy – a guided walk

It may be difficult or costly for you to access specific therapies. Although it is an overused truism, it really is good to talk! Research has proven that in actual fact, the type of therapy is virtually irrelevant. What is important are the characteristics of the person who is delivering the therapy, the quality of the therapeutic relationship and the warmth and empathy extended by that person. With that in mind, it may prove just as rewarding for you to set up regular meetings with someone you trust, who possesses those above qualities and who is prepared to "guide you through the difficult times"

Only divulge and discuss things that you feel "safe" with. Remember that when you are feeling better your friend or family member will still know your intimate details! Good friends "stay" the course but sometimes it can impact on the friendship. For this reason sometimes people feel safer disclosing to someone not especially close to them. Is there a befriending scheme or counselling service that might be more appropriate?

Friends as "Crisis Supporters"

Arrange with a friend the boundaries of telephone contact. Is it acceptable to call up to nine, ten, eleven o'clock at night. Is that person willing to say to you, "In a crisis call me at any time of day or night?" To know that you are able to contact someone at any time often removes the fear and likelihood of you actually needing to do so! Friendship extends two ways, however.

Are you willing to reciprocate the favour? Could you equally "be there" for your friend? Come to a working arrangement between the two of you. If there are no friends or family able to support you in this way, ensure that you have an emergency contact number by your phone – a helpline, the Samaritans, crisis team etc.

Real friends are those who when you make a fool of yourself, don't think you've done a permanent job

"I have learned that to have a good friend is the purest of all God's gifts, for it is a love that has no exchange of payment" – Frances Farmer

A real friend will tell you your faults and follies in times of prosperity,
And assist you with his hand and heart in times of adversity

If I could catch a rainbow
I would do it just for you.
And share with you its beauty
On the days you're feeling blue.
If I could build a mountain
You could call your very own.
A place to find serenity
A place to be alone.
If I could take your troubles
I would toss them into the sea,
But all these things I'm finding
Are impossible for me.
I cannot build a mountain
Or catch a rainbow fair,
But let me be what I know best,
A friend that is always there.
Khahlil Gibran

Healing past and current Trauma
Hearing Voices

Hearing voices is not such an unusual experience as medical psychiatry would have us believe. Indeed 4% of the population would appear to hear voices. Amongst people with mental health problems however the incidence of voice hearing is higher, this is thought to be because people who become mentally distressed have different life experiences, 70% of people with Schizophrenia say that they hear voices that trouble them because of life events .We know that hearing voices is never in itself the problem, rather it is something else which is the problem for people who hear voices and become patients. The good news is we can do something about these things.

What then makes voices a problem? It is the relationships you have with your voices, their identity, how they fit into your life, the power they may have over you and your ability to defend yourself, your understanding and explanation of them, the context in which they arise and how they disrupt your life or others around you and your way of coping that can cause problems (Smith & Coleman 2005)

What can be done? There are many things you can do to help with these things either for yourself or to help someone close to you - understanding the relationship with voices, their origins, the influence they have in a persons life, the disruption they cause, the context in which they arise etc. which collectively we call reforming.

Here is a brief list of things you can do;
* Identify who or what your voices are
* Look at your relationship with them
* Look at the origins of them
* Look at how they have changed over time, the distress they cause,
* How you cope and how else you can cope
* Your understanding and context
* Your social network / disruption.

Coping strategies for Voices may include;
* Replying to the voices
* Designating a set time and duration for the voices
* Dismissing the voices for a certain period
* Writing down what the voices say and want
* Checking whether what the voices say is true
* Creating boundaries
* Postponing orders
* Substituting different orders and learning to express anger
* Anticipating the voices
* Talking to someone about the voices
* Talking into a mobile phone allows you to get out in public and still respond to voices!
* Singing aloud

Self Harm

"Repetitive Self Harm is any purposeful act or omission that results in harm to the person but is without any direct intent to end life and occurs more than once over time"   *Mike Smith (2003).*

Psychiatry in DSM IV (the Diagnostical Statistical Manual) defines self injury as "The deliberate damaging of body tissue without the intent to end life". Clearly, therefore, self harm includes self injury but is a more expansive term.

Self harm and suicide therefore are different things, the key difference being intent. Statistically people who harm themselves are more likely to go on and end their life by suicide but that does not indicate any direct or positive link, especially if life events are controlled. We know that for most people separating their motivations to hurt themselves from any possible motivations to die can be a broadly helpful part of building their future resilience and making choices.

We believe that self harm is a survival strategy that helps the person to make sense of the world and to survive today; therefore we never hope or ask that people will stop unless they feel it is right to do so at this point in their life.

When training workers to build their helpfulness we often start with the following tips;

- **First separate self harm from suicide**
- **Self harm is never the problem so don't focus on it when working**
- **Self harm is a messenger that there is a problem elsewhere, help the person listen to, understand and heed the message**
- **Don't aim for the self harm to stop, aim for the person to have more control or to make choices– and oddly enough it often stops**
- **Recovery from the problem is natural and we know it eventually stops even if we do nothing, so workers should be kind, human and hopeful.**
- **Self harm is not simply about getting your attention; don't over emphasise your importance in your clients lives**
- **One of the biggest obstacles to overcome is workers' and others' hopelessness. It is hard for a person to find their hope when they feel desperate. Workers must be the holders of hope. When workers are hopeless it is hard to raise your own expectations from being a "cutter" to being a person.**
- **Help the person to make sense of what is happening and to make choices**
- **Ownership of the experience is important, workers do not own clients experiences or the recovery process.**

Why do people hurt themselves?
Recent studies have suggested some alarming links between life events and the development of self harm in later life. These links are often recognized and understood by the person who harms themselves, though services do not always explore these connections. Often adults who harm themselves start to self harm during adolescence and the factors of time and history can therefore be an added problem when it comes to building resilience and finding their future again.

In their study Diclemente et al (1991) for instance, found that amongst adolescents in a psychiatric service who reported sexual abuse, 83% cut themselves. This psychic distress is believed to be a common factor which may manifest itself in many ways. The commonest of these ways is in some form of self harm.

"Self injury is quite an obvious response to abuse. The need to "get rid of the filth" is often reported by survivors of abuse who cut themselves to get rid of internalized feelings of shame"

"Defending oneself against owning the abuse and surviving through transferring the pain onto the body – the effect of which blocks intense feelings of emotional pain that would otherwise be un-survivable. This is the symbolic language of self harm. "It is another way of expressing the unspeakable". What words could describe the feelings that go far beyond our understanding of them, but whose power urges their release through the most guttural forms of physical expression as in self injury? Dianne Harrison

Some of the many reasons why a person may self harm include the need

- To survive
- To communicate
- To cope
- To feel better
- To get help
- Transfer emotional pain to physical
- To show I am different
- To belong
- To heal
- To see blood
- To check I'm alive
- To feel something
- I deserve it/punish self
- To punish others
- To dissociate
- To control something
- Or our own favourite---Its complex!!

Workers and others need to stop trying to find simple solutions to complex problems. They also need to separate self harm from suicide attempts in order to truly help the person.

Separating self harm from suicide

In theory, suicide and self harm are easy to separate, but in practice many professionals confuse them. Self harm is about staying alive and feeling better. Suicide is a deliberate act with direct intent to end one's own life. Self harm is not associated with direct suicidal intent, however;

- People who self harm are at risk of accidental death
- People who self harm are more likely to also become suicidal and to complete suicide according to a Royal College Psychiatrist Report June 2003
- Some forms of self harm are more likely to be lethal by accident, recklessness or carelessness; this in itself leads one logically to harm reduction as a way of surviving today whilst one builds your resilience.

Assessing risk

A helpful approach is to assess risk and safety together with the person who commits acts of harm. We have developed a risk assessment tool for workers and for people who self harm to consider the risks and the safety factors together which is called SHARS (Self Harm Assessment of Risk & Safety) This is available free from our website, www.crazydiamond.org.uk

It does not pretend to predict risk, rather it balances the opinions of workers, carers and the focal person and leads to a strategy by which the focal person can mange their own safety. It is based in a consideration of what we see as the 5 domains of self harm

- **Intent** – people who are clear that they intended to stay alive would have a low score; people who are ambiguous or unclear, or have the possible intent to die have a higher score. The discussion around intent can prove useful to all concerned.
- **Directness** – how directly linked are the person's life experiences and emotions to current self harming? People who can relate their self harming to life events and experiences may be safer than those who see no link or have no explanation for why they self harm.
- **Potential Lethality/Damage** – many forms of self harm, despite having no direct intent to end life, can be lethal. In our experience of working with people who harm themselves by cutting, many cut in ways that are less risky for themselves. But some people, particularly those who are impulsive or emotionally explosive may cut in a more potentially lethal way. The use of ligatures and poisoning is potentially more dangerous, although each case must be appraised individually.
- **Control and current distress** – many people have a high degree of control over when and how they self harm, and over the intensity and severity used. They may be judged to be safer than those who demonstrate little or no control or who feel that their self harm is inevitable, particularly if they have a compulsive nature. Control can be significantly affected by current levels of distress and social circumstances and therefore these factors should be considered when assessing the person's ability to control what is happening
- **Repetitiveness** – the frequency of incidents of self harm and any escalation is the final domain to consider. Obviously, frequent potentially lethal self harm is riskier than infrequent and rare potentially lethal self harm. This area has to be considered along with the other domains and is an example of why the domains cannot be separated.

Stages of Surviving

- Begins with a decision to heal
- The emergency stage (Beginning to deal with memories and suppressed feelings)
- Remembering
- Believing it happened
- Breaking the silence
- Understanding That It Wasn't Your Fault
- Making contact with the child inside (Many survivors have lost touch with their own vulnerability. Getting in touch with the child within can help you feel compassion for yourself, more anger at your abuser and greater intimacy with others.)
- Trusting yourself (The best guide for healing is your own inner voice. Learning to trust your own perceptions, feelings and intuitions forms a new basis for action in the world.
- Growing and mourning (As children being abused, later as adults struggling to survive, most survivors haven't felt their losses. Grieving is a way to honour your pain, let go, and move into the present.)
- Anger can be the backbone of healing, a powerful and liberating force.
- Directing your rage at your abuser and at those who didn't protect you, is pivotal to healing.)
- Disclosure and Confrontations
- Resolution and Moving On

What helps?

- Assisting the person to take ownership of their self-harm
- Hope and optimism
- Working through the links between self-harm and past experiences
- Working through any contributory factors – thoughts, feelings around self-harm and whether there are differing parts of oneself - voice hearing, positive/negative relationships etc. may all need to be explored.
- Talking therapy in a group or one to one
- Cognitive or psychological therapies
- Distraction techniques
- Finding a safe place e.g. could be a restful room, in the garden or under the bed
- Drawing on events that give the self-harmer a sense of power
- Developing alliances and agreements to work together (focussing on the self-harmer's experiences and goals)
- Being non judgmental and supportive
- Positive relationships
- Acceptance of the person behind the self-harm.
- Making sense, identifying patterns, owning the experience, understanding the context and links to your life story
- Making choices, building resilience and finding your future

What is unhelpful?
- **Complying with labelling process**
- **Contracts that state help will be withdrawn if the self-harm continues**
- **Fighting to make the self-harm stop**
- **Controlling the person**
- **Being angry or telling the self-harmer off**
- **Making the self-harmer feel bad, insecure or naughty**
- **Giving the self-harmer a guilt trip**
- **Telling the self-harmer they are silly, stupid etc**
- **Stereotypical responses – seeing the person as manipulative, attention seeking or difficult**

Coping Strategies for Self Injury

Why is it that you want to injure yourself? What are you feeling? Are you angry? Wanting to see blood? Depending on your feelings or reasons different substitutes/ distractions may be more useful than others. Below are some suggestions for things to try doing rather than injuring yourself.
- **Play loud angry music**
- **Go cycling until you're worn out**
- **Stab at an old catalogue with something sharp**
- **Get a punch bag**
- **Flick your wrist with a rubber band**
- **Have a cold shower**
- **Do some hard physical exercise (sit-ups or press-ups if you cant face going outside)**
- **Squeeze an ice cube**
- **Play a computer game such as "Tetris" or "Space Invaders"**
- **Play a card game like "Patients"**
- **Clean your house**
- **Watch a film/ read a book**
- **Use red paint to draw on yourself**
- **Draw on yourself with a red ice cube (made with water and red food colouring)**
- **Play a computer game such as "Tetris" or "Space Invaders"**
- **Paint PVA glue on the area you want to injure, let it dry, and then peal it off.**
- **Pluck hairs**

Self harming behaviour is a way of coping with distress. The need to self harm is in fact underpinned by the need to survive. If we understand this then we do not need to be stuck at dealing with the behaviour. We have no need therefore to judge it or the person. We simply need to help them repair the damage in an empathetic way.

Supporting someone who self harms

If you are supporting someone who self harms it is vital that you take care of yourself and don't let your life be taken over by the self harm. Acknowledge and deal with your own feelings and try to build support networks for yourself. Don't assume that you can "rescue" the person, and importantly, don't blame yourself or feel guilty for the person's actions. Remember that this is their way of coping. Most importantly, keep all lines of communication open and help the person to explore the context for their self harm.

False Guilt

If we do something we know to be wrong, most of us would probably experience feelings of guilt as a natural response. However what we refer to as "false guilt" is a common emotion in many people who experience psychic distress. Often it is not through any wrongdoing on the individual's behalf but is linked to past trauma and abuse where the individual struggles to understand that things were not their responsibility or fault. Guilt is something which abusers instill into their victims in order to maintain secrecy and compliancy. By telling the person that it is their fault the abuser can retain his or her own sense of self. So it is not surprising that some adults who were victimized in this way as children grow up with a false sense of guilt and responsibility. That sense of guilt may encroach into other areas and with other people  unrelated to the abuse because those feelings of guilt have been so heavily indoctrinated and they may end up feeling guilty for things other people do or say, without it being anything to do with their own actions or behaviour. Linked closely to this is the inability to forgive oneself which compounds the guilt and prevents you moving on. The following characteristics may be closely associated with "false guilt"

- Low self esteem
- Perfectionist tendencies
- Inability to express emotions easily
- Tendency to become depressed
- Anxiety
- Need to control
- Inability to forgive others
- Fear of making mistakes
- Inability to understand what others see in you
- Constant need for reassurance

Elsewhere in this manual we deal with each of these characteristics but for now it may be useful to consider the following;

- Discuss the areas you feel relate to you from the above list with someone you trust
- Discuss your feelings of guilt with someone you know would be empathetic
- Acknowledge that your guilt may be "false guilt"
- Learn to let go of some of the perfectionist and controlling tendencies
- Write down exactly what you feel guilty about
- What do you think is the root cause, does your guilt relate to a specific person or experience?
- If so, try to "reframe" the experience by looking at it more objectively
- Acknowledge that making mistakes is natural – it's how we learn

"True guilt is guilt at the obligation one owes to oneself to be oneself. False guilt is guilt felt at not being what other people feel one ought to be or assume that one is"   *R.D. Laing*

Forgiveness
"The stupid neither forgive nor forget;
The naïve forgive and forget;
The wise forgive but do not forget"
                    Thomas Szasz "The Second Sin" (1973)

Forgiving others, for some people, may be easier than forgiving oneself. Others will assert that they are unable to forgive other people who have wronged them. We believe this is a personal matter – some people's stories of abuse and trauma are so horrifying that forgiveness may be impossible to even consider.

Yet others do seem able to forgive, as in the case of the family of Abigail Witchalls who was paralysed in a knife attack and the mother and sister of Anthony Walker who was murdered in an unprovoked attack. Gee Walker, Anthony's mother said that she would "follow Jesus' example and forgive his killers".

Forgiveness certainly challenges even those who have a committed faith; it challenges you to give up destructive thoughts about the situation and accept that there may be a moving on process. This realization that forgiveness is akin to giving yourself a gift, may restore health and a more positive perspective on life is one of the reasons Gee Walker and her daughter Dominique were able to forgive Anthony's killers.

"Unforgiveness makes you a victim and why should I be a victim? Anthony spent his life forgiving. His life stood for peace, love and forgiveness and I brought them up that way".

Seen this way, forgiveness can be regarded as an internal matter. It builds confidence that you can survive the pain, grow from it and not allow others despicable acts to destroy your future. There are risks that if forgiveness is not at least worked towards then you potentially remain bitter, vindictive, a victim, allowing the perpetrator even greater power over you. Focus on you, your wellness and recovery.

At the end of the day it is a choice. It may take many years; total forgiveness may never come but by looking to the future rather than constantly reliving the hurt and pain then you allow healing to begin. Non-forgiveness keeps you in the struggle. Being willing to forgive can bring a sense of peace and well-being.

What helps with guilt?
- Acknowledging your own hurt and pain as an understandable response
- Accepting that forgiveness is not the same as condoning what has happened to you
- Realizing that forgiveness has benefits for you
- Seeing forgiveness as part of a healing journey
- Seeing yourself as moving from victim to victor
- Seeing yourself as courageous in your decision
- Expressing other emotions – anger, resentment, sadness, grief
- Drawing on your spiritual or religious beliefs

Flashbacks

Sometimes when people start to deal with issues from the past they may experience flashbacks of certain situations. Flashbacks are powerful reminders of the bad memories, even things long submerged or forgotten. This is perfectly natural and may form part of the healing process.

Flashbacks may take the form of visual experiences / pictures, sounds, smells, body sensations, feelings or the lack of them (numbness). Many times there is no actual visual or auditory memory.

Often these will be accompanied by feelings of panic, powerlessness, loss of control. You may feel trapped.

As we remember past events, the "child" part of us not only remembers but "re-lives" the experience. It is frightening because the feelings and sensations are not related to the reality of the present and may seem to come from nowhere. When flashbacks occur, the "adult" self resorts to the "child" self (powerless, frightened, and confused), so it is helpful to remember that you can bring back the adult self (having choices, having the ability to do something about situations, being in control and powerful)

Things that may help with flashbacks

- Recognise that this is a flashback, you are not going mad!
- Breathe deeply, keep calm, allow yourself time to recover from the experience
- Allow your emotions – it may be that experiencing some degree of anger, fear, crying may be therapeutic
- Bring yourself back into the here and now by focusing on an object in the room or by looking out of a window
- Soothe yourself by rubbing your arm, your legs, neck etc.
- Repeat affirmations to yourself, or preferably out loud
- Tell yourself that what you are experiencing is a memory, it has passed
- You may need to "honour the experience" by naming the emotions it has evoked – rage, disgust etc.
- Congratulate yourself on surviving the trauma

"Like an abandoned house dusty covered
Furniture still intact
If I visit it now will I simply re-live it somehow gratuitous

But who's still aching now?
Who's tired of her own voice?
Who is it weighing down with no gift from time of said healing?

I want to be big and let go of this grudge that's grown old
All this time I've not known how to rest this bygone
I want to be soft and resolved, clean of slate and released
I want to forgive for the both of us

Maybe as I cut the cord
Veils will lift from my eyes
Maybe as I lay this to rest
Dead weight off my shoulders will rise

Here I sit much determined
Ever ill-equipped to draw this curtain
How this has entertained, validated
And has served me well
Ever the victim

But who's done whining now?
Who's ready to put down
This load I've carried longer than I had cared to remember"
Alannis Morrissette "This Grudge"

Panic Attacks

Many people experience panic attacks at some point in their life, and it can be a frightening experience. They may accompany flashbacks or they may come out of the blue and leave people feeling terrified and totally out of control. There may be physical causes or the attacks may relate to life events, childhood influences or even personality traits.

During an attack you may feel a range of symptoms, including
- **Breathlessness**
- **Sweating**
- **Feeling dizzy**
- **Feeling nauseous**
- **Terror**
- **Chest pains**
- **Palpitations**
- **Feeling detached**
- **Feeling that you are going mad**

Sometimes the attacks are so severe that you feel that you are going to die. But it is possible to learn techniques to lessen the fear and become more in control. Understanding what is happening to you is key to overcoming the fear. Some stress and our reaction to it is quite natural – such as going to the dentist for example. However if stress is ruling our lives or there are other problems we may have the same reaction on an ongoing basis or randomly and seemingly inappropriately.

When we are threatened our brain 'tells' our body to produce adrenaline and other related hormones. Adrenaline is the fight or flight hormone. Adrenalin sends blood to the areas which would help us to face the danger or run away from it.

Like a vicious circle the brain, body and mind send messages to each other

The "mother gland" in the brain sends out signals to the adrenal glands to secrete adrenaline. The heart pumps hormones to the limbs and lungs through the circulation of blood. The pulse races, breathing becomes shallow, hands tingle and dizziness may occur. This is the "Fight or flight" scenario which enables us to react to danger by running away or standing up to the situation.

The mind has thoughts and feelings of unreality fuelled by breathlessness and a racing heart, thoughts of fainting, even death. These thoughts drive heightened anxiety so the brain secretes more adrenaline which causes more feelings of fear etc.

This is the vicious circle!

But once you understand this, you can learn techniques to break the circle or as we say, get off the escalator!

Stress can be escalated, i.e. we just keep going up.
Like the Eiffel Tower we don't have to go to the top! We can get off and walk back down.

Get off the thought escalator
Escalate
- I can't breathe
- I must be going to faint
- I'm never going to wake up
- I may even die right here

De-escalate
- I can't breathe
- But I know it will pass
- Even if I faint that will be the worst thing that can happen
- I know I'll keep breathing

Distraction Techniques
Act!
Hold breath or take deep breaths into a paper bag
Stop shallow breathing making your hands tingle / feeling dizzy
Count backwards in 7s from 100
Chew something
Snap a rubber band
Call a friend
Watch T.V.

Fears and Phobias
Like all emotions, although we experience them within our bodies, the emotion of fear is generated in our brains. It tends to be triggered when we are threatened (or think that we might be damaged) in some way. If it pervades our lives in a general way, it can become somewhat debilitating. We can live in anxious fear of something that may or may not happen. A persistent irrational fear of and desire to avoid an object, place, person or activity, is called a phobia.

There are many different aspects of phobias – they may be based on superstition, taboos, ignorance, perceived danger, apprehension, learned association or arise from abuse, neglect or trauma.
Some fears can lead to obsessive - compulsive behaviours. Some people find that systematic desensitization / exposure therapy is useful. Others may gain benefit from Cognitive Behaviour Therapy, Emotional Freedom Technique Therapy, as mentioned earlier in the chapter or just simple relaxation.

HIPPOTOMONSTROSESQUIPPEDALIOPHOBIA
– Fear of long words!

YOU HAVE NOTHING TO FEAR BUT FEAR ITSELF!

Coping with stress / reducing stress in your life

Ways of looking after yourself

- **Eat a sensible diet**
- **Get sufficient rest**
- **Phone a friend!**
- **Pace things out during day so you are not rushing neither are you left with huge chunks of the day without anything to do**
- **Treat yourself as you would a special friend – imagine your special friend was coming to visit. What would you do differently? Maybe make an effort for the house to look nice, buy fresh flowers, cook good food etc. What stops you doing this for yourself each day? It reminds you that you are special, and deserving of being treated well.**
- **Buy yourself a small present**
- **Find a form of exercise which you enjoy – swimming, walking, jogging etc. and try to do it on a regular basis**
- **Develop "winding down" strategies – listening to music, having a bath etc.**
- **Learn relaxation techniques – meditation, yoga etc.**

When we're rushing about, tense and stressed we become like machines / robots. In order to fully appreciate the world around us and the gifts of nature, friendship, kindness etc. we need to slow down. The Buddhists have the approach of savouring and appreciating the whole experience of each activity, being "mindful" of each stage. You could incorporate this approach into your daily life, for example, bathing. That can become a pleasant multi-sensory experience – music, candles, perfume etc.

Try to unwind by using simple breathing and relaxation techniques. The following are simple yet effective techniques that you can do anywhere, anytime.

Relaxation method 1

First of all, sit comfortably and starting with your feet, clench tightly all the muscles, one set at a time, working up through
Feet
Calves
Thighs
Stomach
Shoulders
Arms
Hands
Face
Eyes
Then on the count of 3 relax

Relaxation method 2

Sit comfortably, or lie down if you prefer, feet apart, palms upward
Make a clenched fist; clench it really tight, hold for the count of three, release
Suck in your stomach; try to make it touch your back. Hold for count of three. Release
Clench your teeth, hold for three. Release
Close your eyelids tightly. Press down more and more. Hold for three. Release
Push your head and neck into your shoulders. Down as far as you can. Release
Breathe in deeply. Hold for as long as you can. Release when ready
Stretch out your arms, then legs, then release

Now try all seven steps at the same time!
When really tense, release and imagine a warm, soft wave over your body, relaxing each part in turn, as it slowly moves from your head down over and into every muscle. Let it loosen the tension around your eyes, forehead, mouth, neck and back. All tension out. Relaxation in.

Breathe in and out slowly five times
Imagine yourself in the most relaxing situation possible; e.g.
Floating down river in a raft
Lying on a beach
Soaking in a hot bath
Walking in the woods

Go in to your relaxation image in your mind.
See it, feel it, hear it, smell it and touch it with your mind.
When you are fully relaxed, count to ten, and then open your eyes.
Stretch.

Do this every day or whenever you feel tense.
Keep aware of your stress levels.
Use the following checklist to monitor how you are feeling, and if you feel you are showing signs of high stress ensure you talk to someone you trust and who cares about you.

Checklist of stressful symptoms

Physical symptoms may include;

Muscular tension	Constipation or Diarrhoea
Muscular aches and pains	Breathlessness
Tension headache	Tiredness
Palpitations	Feeling weak
Changes in appetite	Insomnia
Indigestion	

Behavioural signs may include;

Increase in smoking	Reduced level of skill
Drinking more alcohol than usual	Avoiding people
Poor concentration	Loss of libido
Inability to finish things	

Stress related thoughts may include;

Intrusive, unwanted thoughts	Self critical
Worrying obsessively	Critical of others
Inability to make decisions	Lapses of memory

Emotional symptoms

Irritability	Feeling weepy
Anger	Feeling helpless
Resentment	Loss of sense of humour
Loss of temper	Feeling guilty
Anxiety	

Factors to bear in mind
Time factor – how long it takes to reach a pitch
Intensity – How strongly you feel the disturbing symptoms
Durability – Can you stay with the feelings or must you escape?

Which of the following statements represents where you are?

1. I am not very often fearful except on those occasions when it is necessary
2. I am fearful but I can live with the tension
3. This fear is ruining my life! What can I do about it?

If you have identified yourself as being at stage 3, you may need to seek the advice of someone you trust and who cares about you. Talking to an empathetic person may help, and there are alternatives which will help such as yoga, relaxation, some of the therapies referred to elsewhere in this chapter.

Know yourself and what you want
- **Acknowledge, accept, express and share your feelings**
- **Reward your achievements**
- **Learn how you show strain**
- **Monitor your levels of stress / strain daily**
- **Predict periods of stress and plan for them**
- **Be flexible; use the potential for growth in stressful situations**
- **Don't dwell on negative events or comments**
- **Give attention to spiritual development**

Take responsibility for your own life

Who am I?
Try this exercise to see how well you feel you understand and know yourself

1. **I must be loved or at least liked by other people**
2. **I must be perfect in all that I try to do**
3. **When things do not go the way I want them to go I get angry or depressed**
4. **I can have very little control over what happens to me**
5. **It is easier to avoid difficulties than to face them**
6. **I can't change how I am**
7. **People are fragile and we should keep our thoughts to ourselves in order not to hurt them**
8. **Anger is always bad and destructive and should be sat upon**
9. **We should always try to please others without considering our own needs**
10. **We can only be happy when we are with other people**

Remember it is ok to say No!
The words "Should" and "Ought to" are not healthy or useful to you moving on!

Understanding what makes me tick:
Exploring what it is that makes you who you are, learning how others perceive you and the signals you give off may help in your recovery. One of the most common things that people do who have experienced mental ill health is to allow the negative views, ignorance and stigma within the community surrounding mental health to impact on how they feel about themselves.

This is seen often at conferences or meetings where individuals introduce themselves as "just a service user". An assumption that other people are superior because they enjoy good mental health is not only damaging to yourself it is totally unrealistic. We all co-exist on a continuum of health and mental wellbeing, but some people, due to life situations just end up sliding further down the scale!

Don't put yourself down!
Make a list of all the positive aspects of your personality and then the things you feel are not so positive and you could work on.

It is human nature to have the negative list much longer than the positive, and if you are currently experiencing mental health problems your confidence will be knocked anyway so negative words may spring more readily to mind. Compile your list over a period of a few days and be honest but not overly critical.

Now look at your list and think about the second lot of words differently. Are you being too hard on yourself? Ask a friend to help you balance the list out by getting their opinion of what they love and respect about you, and think whether the words in your second list really do apply.
For example;

Positive Traits	Things I need to work on
Generous	Lazy
Loyal	Aggressive
Kind-hearted	Manipulative

Are you really lazy? Or are you just unmotivated? Is medication making you drowsy? Are you feeling physically unwell? Do you consider yourself to be lazy? Or do you simply have a relaxed, chilled approach to life?

Is it that you are truly aggressive? Or do you become easily frustrated, unable to communicate what you really want, being ignored / dictated to by others? Maybe you are just being assertive. Some people find that intimidating especially from females! If anger really is problematic then there are steps you can take to deal with that.

Are you manipulative? Or is it that you are desperately trying to keep some control in your life? Maybe it's that you know what you want and how you intend to achieve it?

It may be that you are putting negative connotations on aspects of yourself that are your potential strengths! Focus on your strengths; continue to work on knowing and accepting yourself.
Don't allow others to put you down!

"Wait a minute man
You mispronounced my name
You didn't wait for all the information
Before you turned me away
Wait a minute sir
You kind of hurt my feelings
You see me as a sweet back-loaded puppet
And you've got meal ticket taste
I see right through you
I know right through you
I feel right through you
I walk right through you
Alannis Morisette "Right Through You"

Encouragement from others

Encouragement from others, particularly when things go wrong is an essential component of recovery. Similarly to holding hope, your supporters should play an important part in encouraging you, building your positivity and supporting your choices.

A fable

A group of frogs were travelling through the woods, when two of them fell into a deep pit. All the other frogs gathered around the pit. When they saw how deep it was, they told the frogs they were as good as dead!

The two frogs ignored the comments and tried to jump out of the pit with all their might. The other frogs kept telling them to stop, that they were as good as dead.

Finally one of the frogs took heed of what the others were saying and gave up. He fell down and died. The other frog continued to jump as hard as he could. Once again, the crowd of frogs yelled at him to stop the pain and just die.

But the frog jumped even harder and finally made it out. When he got out the other frogs said, "Did you not hear us?" The frog looked at them, and explained to them that he was deaf. He thought their shouting at him was encouragement the entire time.

Spend time with positive people!

It is vital to spend time with people who are positive and hopeful for your recovery!

Negativity can rub off on you! Are people genuinely pleased for you when things go well? Are they supportive of your decisions? Or are they dismissive, over-protective?

Success in others can be very challenging to some people who might worry about being "left behind." Do your friends want you to stay exactly as you are? Or do they want you to be the best you can, even if it means losing you?

Be proud of who you are, and how you've grown, and continue to grow. Retain the ability to laugh at yourself – this is always easier when you associate with positive people!

"We have enough people who tell it like it is – now we need a few who tell it like it can be"

Spiritual healing - "Spirituality as a Therapeutic Tool"

Spirituality is increasingly being identified by people with mental health experiences as a vital part of their well-being and recovery from ill health. The search for meaning and the deeply personal nature of spiritual beliefs and experiences are at the very heart of any person's journey – including at times of distress and crisis. What we believe about ourselves, others and the world can have a profound effect on our health and well-being. Our human make up consists of mind, body and spirit.

Human Spirit	**Relates to a higher personal understanding and / or a higher being**
Will, Emotions, Intellect, Soul	**Connects our inner world with the world of others**
Body	**Interacts with the material world through all the senses**

But when the holistic self is fragmented, damage ensues. Damage to the body may be experienced as pain, weakness or sickness. Damage to the soul may be experienced as mental anguish, emotional hurt and paralysis of will. Damage to the Human spirit may be experienced as emptiness, loneliness, meaningless, hopelessness. Our human needs are universal –

- Bodily needs e.g. food, drink, sleep, exercise, etc.
- Safety – I feel secure
- Social - I belong and I can love
- Esteem – I accept me
- Meaning - I understand
- Purpose – I can achieve
- Creativity – I can express and appreciate
- Spiritual – I can reach my potential

It is a pretty scary world out there! How do we make sense of it all?

Exploring meaning and purpose

Many people find that development of their own spiritual beliefs about life can prove helpful to their recovery. Questions such as "Who am I? What am I doing here? Where am I going? What does it all mean?" may be more meaningful when placed within a spiritual or a religious context.

"Many people may ask what is the relevance of spiritual beliefs to someone who is psychically distressed? The answer is simple. To the individual it's a way of life, a last hope for them. If there is spiritual vision it offers people an opportunity to;

- *Evaluate their life*
- *Motivate them for the future*
- *Dedicate themselves to what they believe*
- *Transform their thinking and their way of life."*

Paula Christie, Director Women in Need, UK

Hope looks at the rainbows and not the clouds

There is a rainbow in the soul
For every storm that comes to us-
Faith is our assurance
That the sun will shine again"

The soul would have no rainbow if the eyes had no tears

Exploring meaning, either alone or with others may help you to frame an understanding of your own spirituality. Consider the questions below;

The Spiritual Journey - Questions to ask…
1. Does what I believe make sense to me?
2. Does it bring me peace of mind?
3. Does it help me accept myself?
4. Does it help me live a better life?
5. Does it help me get through the day?
6. Does it bring fulfilment and satisfaction?
7. Does it go someway to answer my questions about the future, about dying, and whether there is life after death?

"You mean I do the Hokie Pokie and I turn myself
around, and that's what it's all about?"

This prayer was found written on the walls of a cellar in Cologne, Germany, where Jews had been hiding from the Nazis.

I believe in the sun though it doesn't shine
I believe in love even though I don't feel it
I believe in God though he is silent

The following may help you on your spiritual journey;

- **Praying for and praying with someone**
- **Expressing emotions**
- **Offloading unhelpful stuff**
- **Asking for help**
- **Seeking guidance**
- **Receiving a degree of healing**
- **Developing hobbies and interests**
- **Find your creativity and promote it**
- **Finding your own personal purpose /meaning**
- **Dealing with factors like anxiety and depression and isolation**
- **Diet**
- **Exercise**
- **Healers**
- **Finding psychological and physical safety**
- **Music – Use it to help you relax, to express yourself (anger, sadness) or as a creative outlet, e.g. learning to play guitar**
- **Help obtained from studying or meditating. Looking at sacred writings, interesting books on spiritual things, courses to fill the mind**
- **Consider the healing force of ritual – rites of passage, worship, using Rosary beads, candles, incense etc.**
- **Consider the strength of communicating – informal chats, support groups, counselling**
- **the therapeutic use of touch**
- **The release of laughter and tears**
- **The use of alternative therapies – aromatherapy, acupuncture, reflexology, etc.**

Chapter 6
The THRIVE© Approach
Resilience

"With a fully armed angel to cover me quickly,
I'm cool under enemy fire.
If I fall, she can crawl right under the wire.

When I'm caustic and cold, she might dare to be bold -
ease me round to her warm way of thinking...
fill me up from the cup of love that she's drinking.
And I find, given time, I can bend like a willow.
She bends like a willow"

Jethro Tull "Bends like a willow"

BEND LIKE THE WILLOW OR BREAK LIKE THE OAK

The elements of Recovery practice are well documented, but the concept remains deliberately vague. There is no definitive point, no time at which a person can say, "I am recovered" and many people would attribute to the idea that we are never recovered, but rather constantly on a journey because there is indeed no end point. Recovery covers a vast range of experiences. For one person recovery may mean a return to work and a good social life. For another, simply getting out of bed, coping with daily chores, and getting to the end of the day may be recovery.

Resilience is a far more meaningful term. It can be an innate quality, the capacity of an individual to cope with trauma and still ultimately thrive. It can also be nurtured and supported by others. Building resilience allows people to see themselves in a new light, encourages self determination, and helps to maintain balance and flexibility to life events thus providing resistance to succumbing to future crises.

It is a term not used widely in mental health circles, but the desire to improve one's lot, turn one's life around, get over being abused, being a victim – this is all part of innate resilience. Sometimes it needs someone to say "You did bloody well to come through that!" When you start to think of yourself in terms of being resilient, someone who did well to get this far, it is much easier to carry on progressing.

What is Resilience?

Some aspects of Resilience may include having spirit, buoyancy, flexibility and the ability to recover from setbacks. Resilience could be described as "The capacity of the person to cope with traumatic events, find personal meaning and move on in life"
Resilience could also be described as the process of struggling with difficulties and disappointments and bouncing back.

It may also be the process of persisting in the face of adversity and is also used to indicate a characteristic of resistance to future negative events. Other components of resilience may include
- The ability to try, acknowledge failure, then try again
- Acceptance of highs and lows as a natural rhythm

The things that have helped you survive may be important coping factors in the future.

Which of the following do you think you possess?
- An inner drive
- A degree of optimism
- Survival instinct
- Sense of self
- Sense of others
- Sense of community / belonging
- Creativity
- Spirituality / personal belief system
- Humour
- Ability to "reframe"
- Flexibility
- Expression of emotions, esp. anger
- Ability to talk about painful events
- Ability to experiment / try something new
- Allowing self to fail / try again

Which are of the most importance to you?

Resilience may be innate, often a factor of survival within us but is also something that can be learned. Have you considered the following?

- Shifting the self image from "damaged goods" to "one who prevails"
- Uncovering the methods for succeeding in the past so they can be duplicated in present
- Providing evidence of capability of meeting challenges in the past so that you can do so again

Having a range of expressions of emotion

It is important for us to be able to express a range of emotions, yet often within mental health systems only certain emotions are encouraged. Some emotions are seen as positive - happiness, excitement, love, joy, peace, etc. whilst others carry negative connotations - anger, fear, disgust, worry, hatred, sadness, etc.

In reality all of these are natural human emotions which make us unique, and there is relevance for each different emotion which may include the following;

- Survival qualities – help us assess situation. Fight or flight situations
- Helps us make contact with our environment, interaction with others
- Foundation of communication – so important in relationships
- Makes us feel truly alive
- Acts as a motivator and helps us achieve certain things
- May indicate when something is wrong or needs attending to

There are a number of myths that pervade and serve to make us ashamed to express ourselves in a different range of emotions;

- That it is a sign of weakness to express emotions
- Only women feel emotions, men use logic
- People grow out of emotions as they get older
- Emotions are inferior to intellect
- Emotions are a sign of neurosis and instability

It is our belief that mental health problems can be improved or worsened by how people are allowed to deal with and express their emotions, many of which may include what could be regarded as "negative" to services but understandable and normal in the context of people's lives.

How do you express yourself?

Take a few minutes to consider the following emotions, and write down the ways in which you do express them (if you do) Discuss with someone you trust who cares about you.

Anger

Fear

Guilt

Anxiety

Hatred

Apologising

Pleasure

Pain

Gratitude

Expressing emotion

Are the ways in which you express yourself healthy ones? If not, can you think of alternatives?
Which emotions do you find especially hard?
Do you know why that is?
It may be worth considering the following resilience factors and assessing which you feel are addressed in your life and which may need further work.

Factors that strengthen resilience

Resilience factors and strategies may include the following components – all of which we have included in this manual. It may be worth reflecting how confident you feel each of these areas are addressed in your life.

- Caring / supportive relationships
- Relationships that create love and trust, provide role models and offer encouragement and reassurance
- Capacity to make realistic plans and take steps to carry them out
- Positive view of self
- Confidence in own strengths and abilities
- Skills in communication / problem solving
- Capacity to manage strong feelings / impulses

10 ways to build resilience

1. Make connections
2. Avoid seeing crises as insurmountable problems
3. Accept change as part of life
4. Move towards goals
5. Take decisive actions to remove obstacles
6. Look for opportunities of self discovery
7. Maintain positive view of self
8. Keep things in perspective
9. Maintain hopeful outlook
10. Holistic approach – meditation / spiritual/an open mind

Write down three ways in which you have recently expressed each of the above components as a checklist that you are working on building your resilience.

At the heart of resilience is a belief in oneself -- yet also knowledge of something larger than oneself. Resilient people do not let adversity define them. They find resilience by moving towards a goal beyond themselves, transcending pain and grief by perceiving bad times as a temporary state of affairs.

Natural resilience

When you feel resilient, what is it about your life that enables you to be strong and to bounce back? Think hard about this one. Sandra Escher a Dutch scientist found that with children who hear voices, resilience was often evident; however there were many obstacles that hindered people's natural resilience. These were commonly things such as anxiety, depression, few friends, practical problems or trouble in their lives.

What gets in the way of your natural resilience?
Make a list
What can you do about the above things?

Reframing the experience

In our book, "From Recovery to Emancipation" there are many such stories from people who have refused to be bound and defined by trauma, ill health and adversity and who would affirm that they have consequently attained a happier, peaceful state of being akin to "survivor's pride."
In the chapter on emancipation we will explore that theme further and look at how moving away from diagnoses and labels is empowering to the individual.

For now moving away from dwelling on the negative and finding your own ways of reframing your experiences will strengthen your resilience. Uncovering themes that are useful to you, developing your strengths and gifts will motivate you to become even more hopeful and increase your expectations of yourself. As you begin to see yourself in a new light so will your pride in yourself, your resourcefulness, determination and bravery develop.

"People tend to cope in two ways, either as "recoverers" or as "lingerers," said Ted Dumas, a post-doctoral fellow at Stanford University who studies chronic stress. "Recoverers actively try to overcome circumstances by exerting personal control. They also develop their ability to predict what's going to happen next.

Recoverers are the people going about their daily lives. They have a strong social network. They're not holding worries in, unresolved. They're talking to people and getting different perspectives.

On the other hand, lingerers tend to prolong stress by ruminating on things, even when there is no longer evidence around them to support their worries. They linger in a state of feeling helpless. Such behavior is dangerous, and can result in irritability, loss of sleep, poor appetite, not being able to relax, feeling hyper-vigilant or having a sense of dampened emotions. When those symptoms interfere with daily life, it's time to see a therapist".

At times it is perfectly natural to feel helpless and lose hope, but as Dumas states, lingering in that state of helplessness will have adverse reactions on our health. It puts us in a no win situation. Learning or acquiring traits of resilience helps put you in a situation where you are not only able to stay in the game but you've also got a good chance of winning!

When patterns are broken
New worlds can emerge

Two men trod the way of life;
The first, with downcast eye;
The second with an eager face
Uplifted to the sky

He who gazed upon the ground
Said, "Life is dull and grey"
But he who looked into the stars went singing on his way

Sometimes building resilience requires that you change how you interact with others around you, their demands on you, and their expectations of you. We speak later of raising others expectations of you in the sense of what you can personally achieve, but it may be that you need to define more clearly what they can expect you to do with or for them.

Learning to say no – resilient to other's demands
Sometimes it seems easier to agree to do something rather than being assertive and saying no. Indeed some people find immense difficulty in disagreeing with someone or refusing requests. However it can be at a cost to your health if you regularly go along with others demands and it may end up being more stressful than if you had simply said no in the first place.

There is a saying, "If you want a job doing, find a busy person", and it may be that people do make demands on you which are inappropriate. There are many reasons why we would find it difficult to say no – we don't want to upset people, we feel obliged to go along with things, we might feel it is a duty to do something for friends, family, school, church, neighbours etc. but only you know your capacities and abilities of what you can achieve and when it becomes overload.

If this is the case, saying yes will not benefit you or others and may be a cause of mental ill health in the long run. Firstly, it is important to recognise that saying no is not a selfish act. By keeping yourself healthy and free of unnecessary stress you can prioritise and devote time to the most important things in your life. Saying no can actually be good for you. It raises your self esteem to make a decision that you have not been cornered into and may free up valuable time for other pursuits. It is also important to recognise that other people do not hold power over you in your decision making. Weigh up which activities and requests you want to be involved in and which you feel obliged to go along with.

Do you struggle to say no? Where or who does that come from? Consider the following statements to determine whether you are able to say no to people.

- I always say yes to other people because I would feel guilty refusing.

- I don't like hurting people's feelings by refusing requests, even if I don't want to do something

- I always seem to be doing things for other people; I rarely have time for myself

- I feel I have to prove myself if someone asks me to do something

- Other people won't like me if I say no to their requests

- I seem unable to get jobs finished before having to start on something else

- There are certain people I can't say no to

- I feel I have to "pass a favour on"

- It seems disloyal to say no

- It is "expected" of me

If you have identified with any of the above, it may be that you need to consider building your resilience and work out strategies for saying no. These may include;

- Working out whether the commitment is long or short term, whether you can realistically fit it in with all other commitments you currently have

- Deciding to keep to original plans – not changing what you had arranged simply to please someone else

- Defer your decision – let people know you need thinking time. Then you can weigh up the pros and cons before you make your decision

- Don't lie, make excuses or invent reasons why you can't do something. Either gently speak the truth when turning people down or use simple techniques such as "Sorry, I'm unable to" without giving any further details. Said with a smile will soften the blow!

Tolerance and Problem Isolation

In his book, "So You Think you're Mad", Paul Hewitt talks about the phase of tolerating certain problems in order to isolate them.

"Not in relation to ignoring or denying the problem, spending energy hiding and avoiding recognition, but in employing this tolerance in a positive way. This kind of tolerance will help you to enjoy healthier well-being whilst still exhibiting and attempting to control the particular problem that you have".

He goes on to say, *"There is no failure with tolerance. Tolerance allows you to continue a relatively normal life while you are building the compassion to exercise steps towards mental well-being."*
By allowing yourself this tolerance, you then raise your conscious awareness of the problem and learn strategies to isolate and deal with it.

How else can we build resilience?

Other qualities which may help nurture or increase resilience include
- **Willpower**
- **Determination**
- **Resolve**
- **Self Control**
- **Self Discipline**

Willpower is the ability and inner strength which enables you to make decisions, handle situations or carry out tasks regardless of pressures, temptations or difficulties which arise, even though a great deal of effort and focus may be required.

Determination is a firmness of purpose, will or intention as in the determination to succeed at something new. It is often determination that sets us on the course of action. Many people we know who have recovered from mental ill health have done so through sheer determination to prove their psychiatrists wrong!!

Resolve implies a steadfastness and tenacity to bring about change, to come to a decision and find solutions to the problem. Ownership of the problem can then be acknowledged which is a huge leap forward in recovery. Self control enables you to manage and organise your life, to be in charge and have power over situations. This is a skill which helps move you on from being a victim of mental ill health to becoming the victor!

Self discipline is the ability to behave in a controlled and calm way even in difficult or stressful times and to reject instant gratification in favor of a delayed higher goal. It manifests as the inner strength to stick to actions or plans in spite of obstacles, difficulties or unpleasantness. It is one of the pillars of success, and bestows the inner strength to direct your energy and attention to your goal, and persevere until it is accomplished.

All the above qualities are a prerequisite to getting on in life – gaining qualifications, gaining employment, and improving your standard of life, but most importantly they aid wellness.

Which of the above would you say you possess?

Try asking your friends and family – you may be surprised by their answers and find that you already possess elements of all of them. Often when people experience psychic distress, their self perception remains negative, even as they recover. Being aware of the different elements may help you to further build on them, thus increasing your long term resilience.

Building your resilience not only increases your understanding and confidence, but provides you with tools to avoid relapse. By strengthening your inner self you can develop a sense of mastery not only over situations that have already occurred, but over those which potentially may arise which ordinarily may cause you setbacks. It may even set you on a different, potentially more fruitful and dynamic path. The psychiatrist Karl Menninger referred to people becoming "Weller than well" as a result of overcoming ill health.

"Not infrequently we observe that a patient who is in a phase of recovery from what may have been a rather long illness shows continued improvement, past the point of his former 'normal' state of existence. He not only gets well, to use the vernacular; he gets as well as he was, and then continues to improve still further. He increases his productivity; he expands his life and its horizons. He develops new talents, new powers, and new effectiveness. He becomes, one might say, "Weller than well."...every experienced psychiatrist has seen it....What could it mean? It violates our conventional medical expectations, so perhaps it is often overlooked and occurs more often than we know. It may contain a clue for better prevention and better treatment".

Problem Solving

One of our favourite sayings is "It's not the problem that's the problem, it's the way you deal with the problem that's the problem". Once you've got your head round this tongue twister, have a think what it might mean and whether it applies to you. Once you recognise the distinction between focussing on the problem or instead choosing to focus on the way you deal with it then you are increasing your resilience.

A friend of ours Steve hears voices which "come in through the top of his head" and at one time prevented him from going out as often as he would have wished. He could have given in to the problem, remained isolated and lonely. Instead he discovered a unique solution – a silver foil barrier on top of his head would give him protection from the voices which bounce off the metal foil. Not wishing to look mad with a pie tray on his head, he simply put his cap over the top. No one looks twice at him wearing his flat cap as he goes about his business. No one realises inside he's got his protective lining.

It is always possible to eventually find creative solutions to problems. You may need support in this and that's where talking to others will broaden your choices. Sometimes we are too close to the problem to see things with the objectivity sometimes necessary to resolve them.

Questioning

An integral part of problem solving is to constantly question. Often in psychic distress we allow others to inform, educate and instruct without questioning our own views and thoughts on the matter. As we will discuss further in the chapter on Emancipation, this complacency often occurs with diagnoses and labelling.

Many people believe what they are told by medics, professionals and workers. In our experience it is those people who do not unconditionally accept what they have been told, but rather work out a system of understanding for themselves who move on in recovery quicker. Our belief is that wellness comes from within – from knowing and accepting yourself. The 5 step process we spoke of in the chapter on Time is incredibly useful in aiding that process.

For some people who have survived psychic distress, their own resilience has been essential to the process of recovery because interventions from other sources have been so negative. Indeed, the very act of questioning can sometimes be perceived by health professionals as an extra symptom! Incredibly, information can often be scant and tends to be skewed to a medical model of care. Some people are not adequately informed on either their medication or the range of alternatives available. There is a widely held assumption by most health professionals that medication is effective, safe and necessary. This is a dangerous assumption.

Medication comes with risks, some long term, some life threatening. Our own findings, having talked to many individuals who consider themselves to have moved on in their lives are that the vast majority of people who recover without reliance on medication tend to do so more quickly and with more stability. Over- reliance on medication can actually impair the recovery process and maintain people in the role of sufferer. That is not to say that medication is never useful. For some it may be necessary where used appropriately – but that is often the problem, it is used inappropriately and for lengthy duration. It may also serve to prevent people from drawing on their own reserves and summoning up personal resources. Some would question what the medication is actually meant to treat!

Questions you may wish to give some thought to –

1. Why is psychiatry given more control over people's lives than any other medical specialty and is the only medical specialty allowed to blame its patients when its prescribed treatments don't work?

2. Why is the media silent about the way the drug companies have orchestrated the emergence of biological psychiatry?

3. Why does the psychiatric profession feel compelled to "treat" people diagnosed as having "schizophrenia" when, after 100 years of clinical experience and research, there is still no proof in the psychiatric literature that what is called "schizophrenia" is a medical disease with demonstrable neurophysiological dysfunction?

The following piece appeared in a recent article in "Asylum" magazine, long heralded as the voice of democratic psychiatry, *"The idea that schizophrenia can viewed as a specific, genetically determined, biologically driven, brain disease has been based on bad science and social control since its inception. If the scientific argument against `schizophrenia' is judged to be won, it remains to take the evidence to the people, to explain and develop the alternatives in the full light of day. This is why the campaign is led by Asylum, the magazine for democratic psychiatry, psychology, education and community development. We believe the time is fully ripe for a paradigm shift across the field of mental distress and that the alternative knowledges and resources are now in place to mobilise for change. No more will we view the scandal where intelligent persons are expected to accept discredited diagnoses for fear of being labelled as `lacking in insight' and having treatment forced on them"*

Paul Hammersley and Terence McLaughlin

Questioning, informing yourself and exploring independent, alternative thinking may help you to build resilience. Often those who experience psychic distress feel like the child who won't be party to the lie of the majority the Hans Christian Anderson's the story of "The Emperor's New Clothes" – speaking out naively, yet truthfully and crushed by more powerful voices.

Questioning your treatment or your diagnosis is not easy, and the accusation is often leveled that you "lack insight". Similarly, there are certain lifestyles, beliefs and practices that don't necessarily fit into a psychiatric tick box of approval. Educating yourself, coming to your own understanding of who you are, surrounding yourself with like minded people or immersing yourself in the more candid literature will give you food for thought and enable your individual views and opinions to emerge. Less like a fish out of water!

Having enthusiasm

Enthusiasm and passion are possibly the most difficult aspects of resilience to sustain in psychic distress and we will talk far more about this in vivacity. Activities and interests that you once found enjoyable can be the very things you no longer wish to take part in, or when you do the enjoyment is no longer there. Some people find this to be true of the things that have previously made up their daily routines - reading, music, T.V. sports, hobbies, going out with friends, cooking, cleaning, gardening etc.

Keeping hope alive underpins the process of finding enthusiasm again, but there are some simple things you can do for yourself to encourage its return. The psychiatrist, psychoanalyst and ethologist, Boris Cyrulnik has developed the concept of resilience in France. He writes,
"The notion of resilience is one which tries to understand how a blow can be absorbed, provoke various reactions and even a rebound. In fact resilience knits together a thousand factors, some being more effective than others. The way one feels about oneself seems to be a dominant factor in ones aptitude for resilience."

The best way for rehabilitation, he has discovered, which can also be a fairly quick one, comes when the person is able to feel differently about his trauma – what we refer to as reframing.

"When once he can speak of it, describe it, think on it, it is then that begins the control of those over-flowing emotions which came with the shock.".
Tell the secret: "All disappointments are bearable if they are shared though to talk about oneself is not easy. Emotional expressions are important: they make links with those who listen; they bridge the gaps, as if the speaker says, "up until now I've talked about the transparent parts of myself, the most sociable side. From now on, telling you my full story, I ask that I be loved for what I am."

"Resilience is more than resistance; it's also learning to live."

We act as though comfort and luxury were the chief requirements of life, when all that we need to make us happy is something to be enthusiastic about.

Charles Kingsley

Breaking the chain of misfortune

How many of you, like us, have received chain letters – the ones that instruct you to do something, then forward the letter to a number of other people. Don't break the chain you are told, as this will inevitably bring you bad luck or misfortune, whilst acting on the instructions will bring you blessings and good luck. Some people feel compelled to act on these letters, even to the point of sending money sometimes, rather than break the cycle and be the person on whom disaster descends. Some people, of course, delete the emails or throw the letter in the bin.

The notion of how you respond (or not) to a letter and that act determining your destiny is bizarre to say the least, yet many people would feel superstitious about it and probably go along with things "just to be on the safe side". Turn the idea on its head, though.

What if by not doing something positive for yourself or making constructive changes in your life you knew you would experience bad luck every single day of your life. Would that make you determined to break the cycle? Often people sabotage their own healing and recovery by deciding to go along the path of least resistance, not realising that it is just as time consuming, difficult and emotionally draining as putting all energies into moving on in life. Resilient people understand that the way to move on is to let go of the past, reframe our view of it or move on regardless.

"Life can only be understood backwards, but it must be lived forwards"
"What lies behind us and what lies before us are tiny matters compared to what lies within us"

> *In a world full of people only some want to fly*
> *Isn't that crazy*
> *Crazy*
> *In a heaven of people there's only some want to fly*
> *Ain't that crazy*
> *But we're never gonna survive unless we get a little crazy*
>
> *Seal "Crazy"*

Burnout, madness, craziness, depression, voices, psychosis, self injury, breakdown – whatever your experience may be a temporary "solution" to the problems, a way of coping with overload and pain, as described in the song above but it can also be a starting point for growth, discovery and new life.

"Madness need not be all breakdown, it may also be breakthrough.
It is potential liberation and renewal as well as enslavement and existential death."
R.D. Laing

Emotional Barriers

Some people who others regard as resilient would not consider themselves to possess any of the qualities and characteristics we have described. That may be because they have got themselves into a pattern of sabotage, which may be kept hidden from others or they are simply unable to regard themselves as winners, victors or survivors. We all put up emotional barriers from time to time – they serve to protect us in situations of uncertainty or fear, but some people can get into patterns of sabotaging their own health and thus block recovery. It may be that you block other people out of your life, exhibit emotions which sabotage wellness or you may put a protective wall around yourself.

Which of the following apply to you?
- Lying comes more easily than telling the truth
- I reject other people before they can reject me
- I come across as hostile to people I don't know
- I get jealous easily
- I manipulate situations
- I prefer to live without interference from others
- I have little interest in intimacy
- I test people out to see if they'll stick around
- I have frequent angry outbursts
- Others would say I'm eccentric
- I'm always tense and anxious around people
- Others would describe me as very changeable
- I have mood swings
- I tend to cling on to damaging relationships
- I'm dependent on others approval
- I can be reckless and impulsive
- I begrudge other people's success
- I can be selfish and haughty
- I often feel inadequate and inferior
- I expect criticism and disapproval
- I worry constantly about being "found out" and rejected
- I avoid friendships and intimacy yet long for relationships
- Sometimes I feel isolated
- I am fearful of ordinary social situations
- Others would describe me as a loner

Using some or all of the above strategies may impair wellness. They are natural survival techniques or reactions when you have been hurt or experienced trauma. But they ultimately damage only you, not other people and will be a huge obstacle to thriving. There are healthier ways of asserting yourself, being discriminating in relationships and gauging other people. In fact by displaying some of these traits, it would be easy within the psychiatric system, to get labelled as having some sort of personality disorder.

These behaviours would probably be seen as the symptoms of mental illness. We don't believe this to be true, we would say these are the consequences of trauma rather than symptoms of a disorder! However, by employing these strategies you are not only sabotaging your recovery but run the risk of causing yourself greater unhappiness and isolation in the long run. It is important to recognise that for yourself and work out the reasons why you may behave in this way. Where did it originate and what can you do about it?

What does resilience mean to you?
Resilience
Is
the elasticity
of the surface of a still lake
That allows the row boat to glide through
it while making only a gentle
creaking dip and splash-

Is
the bravery
Of the first wave
Of the greens on trees
Before they're sure
That winter's really over-

Is
the ability-
of two arms
stretched hard
around a beloved
to then release-
Colleen Cahoun

Boundaries
Maybe you find it difficult to trust people. If people have let you down this is a natural response, you may even attract untrustworthy people to you, but it may be that you need to build up trusting relationships slowly and surely.

Do people really let you down or are your expectations unrealistic. Often people who are hard on themselves are hard on others! Controlling or manipulative behaviour can often arise from insecurities. It can be a safety mechanism and you may not even realise you are behaving in a manipulative manner.

Consider whether the way you treat other people is how you would wish to be treated. Reflect on the boundaries you have with other people – are they appropriate, helpful, respectful, or does the lack of clear boundaries cause you emotional harm? Learning to recognise which are constructive and which are destructive is all part of taking responsibility for our own actions in life, and will strengthen your resilience.

Things which may be detrimental to you include investing excessive amounts of time, money and emotions on a relationship or settling for "second best". Sometimes people who have experienced emotion trauma overcompensate, assume responsibility for others and take on the role of "rescuer". This often occurs when we have a hazy sense of personal boundaries. Knowing yourself and learning the boundaries will encourage successful, healthy relationships. It is important that you are able to be **you** in all your relationships, not an appendage to a partner, friend or family member!

Answer the following questions truthfully to determine how you feel about your relationships choosing A or B as the statement which most reflects your views.

a) I feel independent and complete as a person
b) I feel incomplete without a partner

a) I am responsible for my own happiness
b) I rely on others to make me happy

a) I have open, honest relationships with people
b) I like to play mind games and have the upper hand

a) I respect the differences in opinions my friends may hold
b) I like people who think the same as me

a) I am able to express my needs and opinions truthfully
b) I often go along with what others say to keep the peace even if I disagree

a) I am happy for my friends to have other good friendships
b) I am jealous when my friends spend time with other people

a) I like the fact that my friendships change and develop
b) I don't like changes of any sort in my relationships

Which answers do you consider are healthier? If you have answered mostly A's, you are already aware of what is healthy. If your answers were mostly B's it may be worth reflecting whether these attitudes are helpful to you or are impeding your relationships with others and also damaging your own self esteem.

Unrealistic Expectation of Self / Perfectionism

Sometimes people who have experienced trauma of an abusive nature may be unscrupulously hard on themselves. At each turn they "beat themselves up" and regard themselves as stupid, pathetic and useless. It is possibly a pattern learned as a result of someone else belittling, disparaging, criticising, punishing, ridiculing, manipulating or even abandoning the individual so that they come to think of themselves as "not good enough".

Try a little harder
You've got to measure up
And make me prouder
How long before you screw it up
How many times do I have to tell you to hurry up
With everything I do for you
The least you can do is keep quiet
What's the problem ...... why are you crying
Be a good boy
Push a little farther now
That wasn't fast enough
To make us happy
We'll love you just the way you are if you're perfect   *Alannis Morissette "Perfect"*

This can also cause people to have unrealistic expectations of others. By placing people initially on a pedestal where they can do no wrong, you set yourself up for disappointment when you discover that they are only human and make mistakes just like everyone else!

As with the thought escalator exercise in the chapter on Healing, it is important to recognise that you are able to stop yourself descending into the pattern of self loathing that can arise from an unrealistic and negative expectation of self. In the chapter on Emancipation we look at raising positive expectations of yourself, but for now consider the following example.

Key to remembering perspective!

This is an example of how easy it is to take a specific, for example, burning the dinner, and turn it into a sweeping statement which increases negative feelings and thoughts about yourself.

In negative thinking, "I burned the dinner" becomes "I always burn the dinner" becomes "I'm useless at cooking anyway" becomes "I can never do anything right" becomes "I'm useless"

Our suggestion is (apart from forgetting dinner, making a sandwich and having a glass of wine) is to stop the thought process developing by refusing to generalise and refusing to start the subsequent thoughts with the word "I". So, the process would go something like;

"I burned the dinner" becomes "It really doesn't matter in the scheme of things that I've burned the dinner" becomes "There are far more important things to worry about than a burned dinner" becomes "Why would I let a burned dinner upset me!" (Then have the glass of wine or beer!)

This way of thinking is akin to the Emotional Freedom Technique Therapy which we mentioned in the chapter on Healing and you may really benefit from learning the tapping techniques for yourself.

Sensitivity as an aid to resilience

Sometimes people who experience psychic distress find that they develop a heightened sensitivity and become stimulated or over aroused by certain situations. They may react strongly or negatively to things others say or do, and become emotional as a result, they may be uncomfortable in crowds or noisy places, becoming disturbed by glaring lights, loud music etc. and some people may develop an acute sense of atmospheres picking up on strong odours, clutter, chaos etc.

This is perfectly natural at times, as psychic distress seems to put some people strongly in touch with deeper levels of consciousness and awareness. Unless feeling like this causes you undue distress, in which case our techniques for reframing and de-escalating the situation may prove useful, simply accept the process as a learning curve which will increase your ability to become resilient in the long run.

Do any of these apply to you?
- I startle easily
- I dislike sirens, alarms or buzzers intensely
- I can get emotional easily
- Other people's moods really affect me
- I dislike people observing me doing things
- I feel uncomfortable in noisy places
- I avoid violent films or television programmes
- I am deeply moved by visual images
- Music can move me to tears
- I sometimes feel totally and utterly overwhelmed
- Certain odours provoke a strong reaction in me
- I react adversely to coarse fabrics or textures
- I sometimes have the need to withdraw into a silent, dark room to get some privacy and relief

If you identify with quite a few of the above statements, then you may be a highly sensitive person. Unfortunately in our culture this is sometimes perceived as a negative trait, especially for men. However, instead of seeing your sensitivity as a flaw, there are some benefits associated with being highly sensitive.

Often, highly sensitive people are much more in tune with not only their own emotions, but also with how others are feeling. Deep thinking, reflective, good ability to learn and conscientious are just some of the positive traits ascribed to those of a highly sensitive nature. In fact, although some people would consider themselves disadvantaged, this trait of character is a helpful aspect of resilience. Some would say it's healthier to express emotions easily rather than bottling them up, and a heightened sense of awareness, good gut feelings, can serve as a protecting factor.

"It doesn't take a talent to be mean
Your words can crush things that are unseen
So please be careful with me, I'm sensitive

I have this theory, that if we're told we're bad
Then that's the only idea we'll ever have
But maybe if we are surrounded in beauty
Someday we will become what we see
'Cause anyone can start a conflict
it's harder yet to disregard it
I'd rather see the world from another angle
We are everyday angels
Be careful with me 'cause I'd like to stay that way"

Jewel "I'm sensitive"

Chapter 7
The THRIVE© Approach
Interdependence

"Interdependence is and ought to be as much the ideal of man as self-sufficiency. Without interrelation with society he cannot realise his oneness with the universe or suppress his egotism. His social interdependence enables him to test his faith and to prove himself on the touchstone of reality"
Mahatma Gandhi 1929

Often in mental health circles we hear of "independent living" or "independence" as if that is what we should be striving for. This is an anomaly as none of us are truly independent of each other. We are interlinked, intertwined and interwoven – that is the nature of society.

No man is an island, entire of itself;
Every man is a piece of the continent, a part of the main"
John Donne 1572 -1631

Society can be thought of as a contract, an agreement or partnership. Therefore we are all interdependent, and despite a certain politician's statement that "There is no such thing as society, there are individual men and women and there are families" (1982) we all hold individual responsibilities and exist in a social context.

Therefore our problems exist in a social context. Some would also note here that madness exists in societies and as a consequence of society not in individuals. People, events, others can drive you toward madness as they also drive you toward sanity.

This can result from "societal denial" of the consequences of events that occur in our society such as sexual abuse, domestic violence, neglect, enforced prostitution, forced marriages and genital mutilation. It can also arise from the dynamics and pressures within dysfunctional relationships. When people have experienced abuse trauma it can be difficult to engage with others and trust again, but interdependence is about learning to connect to others - moving beyond just "me", and looking outwards to friends, lovers, work colleagues, pets, children, and community. Being needed by others and being of service is reported by many to be important in helping themselves and aiding recovery.

"The turning point for me was when I happened to meet and befriend some young people who were homeless, far worse off than myself, but who I could see were not victims of their circumstances. They had vivacity and embraced life and that humbled me. I started doing voluntary work with various organisations working with homeless people and ended up running the Big Issue Office in Coventry." Marion

Interdependence is a two way thing – we give, we receive. The benefits may not be instantly apparent, but once the effort is made to connect with others, to take on a role, to commit to responsibility of some sort, the returns are far greater than the investment!!

One of the prerequisites to good health is the ability to feel connected with others. This extends beyond our inner, intimate circle of people who we love and who love us, but embraces a wider group of people who we feel connected to in some way. This could be through a shared passion, e.g. a sport, music, cinema, theatre, educational courses or through a shared bond or experience.

What do you enjoy?

There are a considerable number of events, many of them free, held in museums, pubs, schools, universities and colleges, churches and cathedrals, parks and community centres. There are sure to be activities which appeal to you but you may need to spend time checking out what's on, where the venues are. Often in psychic distress we find it difficult to make the effort to spend time with other people doing the things we enjoy (or used to enjoy) but taking one step, making the effort to connect again really does improve health and nurture recovery.

List the things that you are passionate about in your life, e.g.

Interests
Hobbies
Pets
Politics
Humanity
Green Issues
Arts
Poetry
Beer

Are you able to enjoy these things as frequently as you would wish? What could you not live without?

Are there things that you used to feel passionate about but your illness has made them take a back seat?

What have you never done but would love to try?

Depression and illness can make us feel that those passions, skills, interests have disappeared. For some people they may prefer to "let them go" as part of the past, move on and discover new areas of interest. For others, it is useful to consider how you might tap into those enjoyable things which are still there under the surface – they might just require patience and time to re-emerge. Rediscovering skills and strengths can be empowering to recovery.

Looking at your support systems

It may help you to identify your circles of support, that is, the range of people who are in your life in different capacities who make up your support network. Don't worry if you have fewer people in your intimacy and friendship circles and more in your association or exchange circles. This can be quite common for many people and particularly for those struggling with mental distress. Remember that things change over time, so it is only a snapshot of where you currently are, but may be helpful to reflect on.

The challenge is to build up more relationships to go into the inner circles and determine which of the paid/ exchange relationships are necessary or essential to your wellbeing. Often people in psychic distress fall into a pattern of accepting help and support from a range of mental health professionals and organisations without considering the vast assortment of opportunities that may exist in their own communities.

My relationship map

Draw a large circle, spiraling out from the centre with 5 areas. Number them from 1-5 with 1 in the middle, then write the names of the following people in the appropriate areas 2-5. You are number one!!

1. **The focus person - you**
2. **The circle of intimacy for loved ones and those especially close to you, for example best friend, family members**
3. **The circle of friendship for good friends, pals, and mates you can count on**
4. **The circle of participation or association for co-workers, those with whom you share an interest or whom you meet for an activity, for example a club or church you attend**
5. **The circle of exchange for the people whom you pay to be in your life or offer you a service, for example the milkman, hairdresser or professionals who currently help you such as counselors, therapists, nurses etc.**

The point of this is that we try to attain a balance of people across the circles, so that our lives don't revolve just around people who are paid to be in our lives! Don't worry if that is how it appears at the moment, just see it as an area that you need to pay attention to.

Questions to ask yourself about your support network

1. **Am I happy/ satisfied with all the people in my support network?**
2. **Do I want to increase certain circles – intimacy / friendship?**
3. **How do I achieve this?**
4. **What changes are necessary?**
5. **Who are the people who are most / least important in my life?**

Peer support

Many people who develop mental health problems receive and in turn offer peer support, i.e. using their experience of distress to help others. Supporting others and receiving help and support from our peers, people who have similar experiences, can be particularly helpful and meaningful. Learning from others who have trodden the path or who are also trying to find their direction can be particularly inspirational and supportive.

Think of a relationship that has pushed you forward and challenged you positively. What were the characteristics of that relationship and the other person? What was it that contributed to your learning and growing from this relationship? The things that people often tell us are significant to them are trust, respect, being stretched, honesty and being challenged. Write down the characteristics that are important to you.

One of the best ways of getting someone to help you is to help others yourself, getting out there and helping others can be positive on many levels as we discuss elsewhere.

"To know that others have walked a similar road
May not make the difficulties or the journey easier,
But should give us hope"

Who cares about you? Do you allow it?

Sometimes psychic distress warps our view of situations and negativity towards ourselves can affect how we think others feel about us also. It is important to place things in perspective and keep a balanced view of how others care for us.

Sometimes we have unrealistic expectations of how others should treat us; sometimes we have a fear of becoming too close or intimate with others. For example, it may be unrealistic for people to visit or phone daily, but equally if we never hear from people for months on end can they be considered close friends? It may be difficult to allow yourself a degree of intimacy, but equally you may miss out on wonderful relationships if you don't take some risks.

"Intimacy is an exposing experience. Exposure reveals our fragmented natures; inner hurts and insecurities, weaknesses we cannot master, a meanness of spirit that degrades us yet binds us"
Clare Thompson

Social Situations

Some people experience discomfort in certain social situations, and this can be exacerbated for people who have experienced mental health problems. Very often we lose the confidence we had before becoming unwell, and it is hard work to recapture it. As we have mentioned previously, our social circles can sometimes diminish and even simple things we may have previously taken for granted become somewhat of an ordeal. Don't despair, though. Many people who have stated that they have previously been "at rock bottom" have managed to come through that ordeal and build up a social life even from zero!

And, importantly, there are no "normals" – simply what is right for you. What one person can do with ease – for example walking into a pub or café alone to meet a friend another would feel unable to do.

The following questionnaire looks at what your areas of difficulty are and will help you to identify problem areas that may need to be solved. Take your time filling it in and don't worry if there are lots of areas of great discomfort.

It may prove useful to discuss your answers with someone you trust and who cares about you.

Rate the following questions using a scale of 0-4

0= no discomfort

1=slight discomfort

2=moderate discomfort

3=great discomfort

4=I avoid this situation

1. Walking down the street alone
2. Going into shops
3. Going on public transport
4. Going into pubs
5. Going to parties
6. Mixing with people at work
7. Making friends your own age
8. Going on a date
9. Being with a group of men and women your age
10. Being with a group same sex and age as you
11. Being with group opposite sex to you
12. Entertaining people in your home
13. Going to a restaurant
14. Going to a disco
15. Being with older people
16. Being with younger people
17. Going into a room full of people
18. Meeting strangers
19. Being with people you don't know very well
20. Being with friends
21. Making the first move in a relationship
22. Making decisions about where to go with friends
23. Being with just one person rather than in a group
24. Getting to know people in depth
25. Taking the initiative in keeping a conversation going
26. Looking people directly in the eye
27. Disagreeing with what someone else is saying and putting your own views forward
28. People standing or sitting very close to you
29. Talking about yourself and your feelings in conversation
30. People looking at you

It is important to recognise that many people would have difficulty doing some or all of the above at certain times, it has less to do with your health problem rather it is the lack of confidence and esteem resulting from psychic distress, therefore you have the ability to reframe and do something about it. Firstly, you have choices – no one should force you into situations you feel totally uncomfortable with, and difficulties with some of the above may not preclude a good social life.

However, if you have difficulty with many of the above areas, it may prove useful to reflect upon this and consider whether it is impinging your happiness, your ability to make friends and your feelings about yourself. If this is the case, talk it over with someone you trust and who cares about you.

What community do you belong to? Do you feel you belong?
It is sometimes useful to draw / represent visually the area in which you live and identify the amenities and buildings you use locally. It can show what is important to us in our neighbourhood and whether we feel we belong.
Draw a map of your neighbourhood – your home and its position in relation to other places you use or visit.

Include the following information on your map;
- Where is your home?
- Where are the places where you meet your close friends?
- Where do you spend the bulk of your time? Home / Job / College / Day Centre?
- What leisure activities do you enjoy?
- Which services do you use? Shops/ library/ bank/ post office etc.
- What transport links are available?

How large is your zone? Does everything you do in your life revolve around your immediate neighbourhood? Everyone is different; some people like to venture further afield, some prefer to stay in their own environs. What is important is that you have a choice and the opportunity to strike out if you so desire.

1. What is your emotional response to your community map?
2. How do you feel about each of the places you have identified?
3. If you could, would you change your map?
4. What changes would you make?
5. Where would you make them?
6. Membership - what's available and how do you "join"
7. Social networks – are they local or further afield?

If you are content and fulfilled by your map that's great. If you are less sure that the current situation is satisfying it may be that you need to look further afield. Consider the following questions;

1. If you had the opportunity to learn something new what might you be interested in?
2. If you had the opportunity to participate in leisure activities what might you be interested in doing?
3. Could you do voluntary work? What type of volunteering would you enjoy?
4. Could you consider part or even full time employment? What might you be interested in doing?
5. If you had the opportunity to expand your social life, what might you be interested in doing?
6. If you had the opportunity to become involved in any groups, what might you be interested in?

What is available in your community?

Often we are unaware of the huge range of activities and opportunities that are on our doorsteps, in the very communities we live in. This may occur for a number of reasons. Some organisations do not have the funding or capacity to advertise themselves widely. There may be misconceptions by local residents of the services or activities on offer or just a reluctance to try something new.

Particularly when you have experienced mental health difficulties there may be nervousness and apprehension at taking part in local events. Maybe you're not sure what to expect.

Within many localities you will find offers of practical help and support as well as leisure and educational opportunities at low cost or even free. Health Centres, community colleges, adverts in local newspapers, local government offices, phone books, churches and libraries are all an excellent source of information of what's on in your area.

These are the "normal" aspects of life which will engender recovery as they give you a broader outlook on the world, create a feeling of being valued and respected, take our place within the community, challenge and stimulate us to keep on trying something new.

Consider the following
We have taller buildings… but shorter tempers; wider freeways… but narrower viewpoints.
We spend more… but have less; we buy more… but enjoy it less.
We have bigger houses… and smaller families;
More conveniences… but less time.
We have more degrees… but less sense; more knowledge… but less judgment;
More experts… but more problems; more medicine… but less wellness.
We have multiplied our possessions… but reduced our values.
We talk too much, love too seldom… and hate too often.

We have learned how to make a living… but not a life.
We've added years to life… but not life to years.
We've been all the way to the moon and back…
But we have difficulty crossing the street to meet the neighbours.
We've conquered outer space… but not our inner space.
We've cleaned the air… but polluted the soul.
We have split the atom… but not our prejudice.
We have higher incomes… but lower morals.

We've become long on quantity… but short on quality.
These are the times of tall men… and short character;
Of steep profits… and shallow relationships.
These are times of world peace… but domestic warfare.
These are days of more leisure… but less fun;
Of more kinds of food… but less nutrition.
These are days of two incomes… but more divorce;
Of fancier houses… but broken homes.

We can choose to ignore these sad facts of life…
Or we can choose to make a difference.

Anon

Chapter 8
The THRIVE© Approach
Vivacity – Feeling Alive

"I'm gonna live my life.
Shining like a diamond, rolling with the dice,
Standing on the ledge, show the wind how to fly.
When the world gets in my face,
I say, have a nice day".

Bon Jovi

"The delight of opening a new pursuit, or a new course of reading, imparts the vivacity and novelty of youth even to old age". Isaac Disraeli

Vivacity, that feeling of really being alive and having a purpose to be here, to carry on with passion, can remain elusive even when people feel that they have recovered from mental health difficulties. There is no denying that it is difficult to retain a positive outlook in a world that many find incomprehensible.

A friend of ours puts things in perspective by reminding himself that for every newspaper headline that flags up an assault or murder by one person, the news that doesn't get reported is that millions of people went about their lives peacefully today, helping others, living well, and choosing to do good. In the same way, the media may flag up the negative aspects of mental ill health, (the mad, bad Schizophrenic approach) but omit to write about the millions of people who recover fully, reclaim and get on with their lives quietly in a number of roles and functions in society.

A number of factors will help achieve this vivacious state of being. Resurrection of interests and hobbies, enjoyment in new activities and friendships is helpful. Enjoying simple pleasures, walking along the canal path, walking in the country, sitting in the park – we all have our own individual pleasures. One of the things in common cited by those who have moved on in their lives is that they have developed a range of coping strategies and resources which enables them to deal with difficult periods, times of stress etc. Others talk about the importance of being in a valued role – for Marion the turning point, after a period of depression and inactivity, was working with homeless people. Some of our colleagues have spoken of the importance of studying at college or university. It seems to be that finding purpose and meaning to one's day is the motivator and incentive to live life vivaciously!

What is Vivacity?
Vivacity or Vivaciousness encompasses a natural vigour for life, a spirited approach that embraces the vital force of being alive. It could also be said to be having tenacity and hope for life and living.

We all have the choice to merely exist or to actually embrace life, but sometimes negative thinking and lack of perspective ties us into the former. This in turn leads us to deny ourselves simple pleasures and valuing ourselves, then the greater pleasures of life become something we choose to repel.

Consider the following questions;
1. Do you turn down opportunities or invitations on a regular basis?
2. Do you dislike being alone but rarely invite others to your home?
3. Do you always expect the worse to happen?
4. Do you want to be loved but are too afraid of being hurt?
5. Do you feel guilty that you are "not good enough", "not doing enough?"
6. Do you deny yourself small treats?
7. Do you feel as if you drive away your friends and end potentially helpful relationships?
8. Are your relationships with other people unfulfilling?
9. Do you regard yourself as "a victim", "someone who is ill and unable to achieve better things?"

If you have answered yes to several of the above, ask yourself why? What is stopping you from embracing opportunities, being with friends, letting negativity steal the years? Why should you feel guilty for treating yourself well? Does it hinge on the last question? Are you seeing yourself as a victim? Someone whose illness prevents living life to the full? If so, it's a little like having money in the bank and moaning that you're poor because you can't make the journey there to draw it out!

A friend of ours, Vanessa Al-Joudi told us,
"I could sit here and take all my tablets and die. Or I could end up in a mental hospital going barmy. Why? Mental hospitals just make you more barmy!I want to be in control of ME. I don't want to be a "cry for help", "poor Vanessa", I don't want to be a victim. I want to be Vanessa who's, yes, been abused, seen her mum murdered, seen all the shit. But I will never kill myself over a man, not even over my mum being murdered. I want to be strong, back in control. I want to LIVE my life."

Vanessa's story is documented in our book, "From Recovery to Emancipation". She speaks frankly of being systematically sexually abused from the age of seven, how the person she always believed was her mother was murdered brutally and her shock at finding the body dismembered. However she refuses to see herself as a victim and like millions around the world, is testimony to the fact that in all of us we have the ability to thrive, however damaging our experiences may have been. A famous quote states "Yesterday is history. Tomorrow is a mystery. Today is a gift. That's why it's called the present".

Think of what you have rather than of what you lack.
Of the things you have, select the best and then, reflect how eagerly you would have sought them if you did not have them."
Marcus Aurelius (121-180)

There is, here and now, much to appreciate. There is life itself with friends, family, and everything that is naturally before us. We just have to look around and take it in. The happiest people are those who set store by these things rather than material goods, success and status. Perhaps it is time to make a list of all the good things we have to be grateful for. So enjoy yourself today because it is not coming back.

"God grant me the serenity to accept the things I cannot change, the courage to change the things I can, and the wisdom to know the difference."

"The secret of health for both mind and body is not to mourn for the past, not to worry about the future, not to anticipate troubles, but to live the present moment wisely and earnestly."
Buddha (BC)

Life's Pleasures

We all have our life's pleasures. Some are common and some are personal. Here are some of ours, what are yours?

Mike	Marion
A spring day	Singing along to the car radio (sad, I know!)
A good beer	Cold Chardonnay on a hot night! (Or any night)
A rugby match	Shopping – not necessarily buying
Cycling in the sun	Museums & art galleries
Cycling in the rain	Exploring a new city
Lying in a tent in the rain	A smile from a baby
Watching a tree	King Prawns
Abdul's chicken kebabs	A hot bath, candles and music
Smelling the sea	Watching the Simpsons with my son
Sailing into Douglas harbour	Spending time with true friends

Do you allow yourself pleasures? If not, why not? Do you not deserve them?

Swimming in pleasures or drowning in shite!

Make an effort. Look at these pleasures when you need to find your future or when you are wondering "Why is it worth it?" It's worth it because, yes life can be shite, but it also has its pleasures. Hopefully your pleasure pool will be deeper than your pool of shite, if not you'd better start finding your pleasures, because often you can do little about the shite, and who wants to drown in that?

When we become psychically distressed, simple pleasures can all too often be overlooked.
Conversely it is in appreciating the simplest of pleasures that draws us back to recovery.

- Being given a hug
- A smile from someone you don't know
- A smile from someone you love
- Finding lots of letters on your doormat and not one of them a bill
- Newly fallen snow
- Receiving a gift
- Giving a gift
- Looking out to sea
- Seeing new born lambs
- Laughing until it hurts
- The smell of newly mown grass
- Chocolate
- Watching a traffic jam from a train

Find a purpose

To obtain a healthy purpose in our lives we need a balance of work, recreation, and relaxation. Depending on how we fill our days, they can be interminably long or they can fly by. Often in our mental distress we isolate ourselves or tend to stick to mixing with others in the same position, and then as we recover we find that has become the pattern.

Many people speak of the support they have received from using day centres and support groups, and often the friendships formed are for life. Indeed some people may find such supports help build up their vivacity, and there is no doubt that being with others who have similar experiences is healing, but vivacity also encompasses challenging ourselves to reach out further and further all the time, embracing life's opportunities.

To use day centres as a stepping stone back to health and life may be vital for some, but if that becomes the only ongoing interaction we run the risk of institutionalising ourselves and limiting the person we can be.

Fresh air
Free, abundant and better than any medicine to immediately lift the spirits!

Walking
Walking around the town or to the shops will do you some good, but there is nothing so certain to improve your wellbeing as getting out and feeling the earth beneath your feet. A local park is better than nothing, but if possible head out to walk in woods, up hills, along the canal banks, by the river.

Helping others
Helping other people can prove effective in recovery. Showing kindness to others is usually a rewarding experience, both to the recipient and the giver, and is a form of therapy in itself! It enables us to get a wider perspective of others, ourselves and the world and provides the "feel good" factor in our lives. It improves our general wellbeing, reduces stress and most importantly gives us a valued role.

"When you are good to others, you are best to yourself."
- Benjamin Franklin (1706-1790)

Animals / Pets
Being with and responsible for a pet can be very therapeutic and activating. It is said that stroking animals lowers blood pressure and makes you calmer and more peaceful. Taking responsibility for another living creature can also be a catalyst for recovery – you have to get out of bed to feed the cat or take the dog for a walk! There is something to be said for the affection an animal shows you – they seem to know instinctively when you're feeling down and best of all they love you when you don't.

Interests and Hobbies
Vivacity is about meeting new challenges, trying new things – whatever your age!

Which of the following have you done? Which would you like to take up?

Football	Absailing	Hockey
Singing	Snooker	Martial Arts
Keep fit	Bingo	Sailing
Theatre	Acting	Bowling
Cinema	Horse Riding	Cricket
Dancing	Model making	Pool
Rambling	Weight training	Squash
Archery	Badminton	Darts
D.I.Y.	Table Tennis	Drama
Fishing	Climbing	Sports
Music	Dominoes	Swimming
Golf Camping	Climbing	Rugby
Tennis	Yoga	Aromatherapy
Cycling	Orienteering	Athletics

Often the cost of maintaining a hobby is prohibitive, although some of the above are inexpensive and easily accessible. It may be worth considering the Direct Payment route, whereby you dictate the terms and conditions of how your money allotted for social care is actually spent. A "broker" enables you to access the activities you enjoy, the places you wish to visit or where you wish to live and assists you in making the financial arrangements, taking an agreed percentage as a fee.

Direct payments and self directed support
Direct payments increase the choice and control that people have over the support they receive. The take-up of direct payments by people experiencing mental health problems has been extremely low in most parts of the country. Local authorities now have a duty to offer direct payments to people who are eligible and to make payments to those who want them. Direct payments offer greater independence and flexibility in support arrangements and, for people from black and minority ethnic communities; this can mean improved access to culturally sensitive support. For people experiencing mental health problems direct payments can facilitate social inclusion, through providing support to access mainstream opportunities.

"Direct payments have been framed in terms of support (not illness or incapacity); in terms of ensuring that people can have the kind and amount of support they need to live their lives as fully, as freely, and with as many choices and opportunities as they can. They can have more choice; they can have more control; because they can with help and independent guidance get the kind of support and assistance they need to live their lives." Professor Peter Beresford, Centre for Citizen Participation, Brunel University

Have your say – "Lived Experience"

Across the country are a number of working groups run by and for people who have experienced mental health problems and this can prove helpful in your recovery. It enables you to link with like minded people, but also gives you an opportunity to have your voice heard as often these groups relay information to providers of services on how to make improvements to the service.

Some people find it helpful to their own recovery to get involved in working in the mental health sphere using their own lived experience as a way of helping others or informing mental health policy and practice. The three main types of involvement are

- Consultation – This is a way of seeking service users' and carers' views on services provided by a Trust or organisation (e.g. on service changes, service quality and service improvements).
- Volunteering - A way of obtaining expert information or advice on the user perspective from a person or group of persons, for example through focus groups, implementation groups, service planning meetings, recruitment panels etc.
- Employment as someone with "lived experience" of mental distress. Often this is in the form of relating your personal story to groups of professionals or more formal training to staff

There may be difficulties in receiving "meaningful" payment for your expertise, this varies around the country and from organisation to organisation but many people have been able to gain employment or become self employed using their lived experience. A friend of ours, Mary Nettle is a mental health service user who now acts in consultation on developmental projects within mental health services. She is a local commissioner for the Mental Health Act Commission and advises researchers who want to involve service users in their work, as required by most funders.

In her paper, "Employment Needs of People with Mental Health Problems" she outlines some of the problems faced by people with mental health problems wishing to return to work;

"The current rate of unemployment for people with mental health problems is 70-80%. This, I feel, is not because people do not want to work, but that current work structures are not flexible enough to accommodate the up and down nature of peoples' emotional lives.

Prejudice (stigma) and ignorance means employers reject people with a history of mental illness. This causes people to lie about their medical history and therefore have no support if they need time off work often leading to them being dismissed from their job.

Particularly in Northern Europe the Social Security system provides a minimum income for people unable to work, but the rigid, inflexible way in which the rules are enforced can lead to what in the UK is called the Benefit Trap. This means that if you are able to get a job you have to give up all your benefit, which may be worth more than the job pays, and, if you find the job is too stressful and have to give it up, you spend a lot of time waiting, often with no money at all, to be able to get the level of benefit you had before".

Laughter

If life seems jolly rotten
There's something you've forgotten
and that's to laugh and smile and dance and sing.
When you're feeling in the dumps
Don't be silly chumps
Just purse your lips and whistle - that's the thing.
And...always look on the bright side of life...."
From "Life of Brian", Monty Python

Laughter doesn't come easily during periods of psychic distress – although many people learn to develop dark humour to get them through. But if you can learn to see the funny side of things it will aid recovery and encourage the quality of vivacity. Remember the thought escalator in a previous chapter – with practice you can jump off with ease! Laughter really is the best medicine of all because it releases other pent up emotions, and represents total freedom of expression. You can't be angry for too long with people who make you laugh, it diffuses anger and bad feelings and sets things right again.

It's often quoted that it takes more muscles to frown than it does to smile – the same could be said of feeling down or miserable. It actually requires a lot of effort and drains us more completely to be unhappy than to go with the flow of learning to be happy and vivacious in life. It can also be addictive. Sometimes we become so accustomed to misery it pervades the soul. The way we stand, the way we sit, the vibes we give out to others, the way we shut off from receiving good things from other people. The more this becomes the norm the more we shrink into this world of negativity. To break free, give attention to these things. Stand upright and proud and straightaway you feel more that way! Find something to laugh at every day and that's what becomes the norm!

Inner Strength

Vivacity comes from an inner strength that keeps you growing despite adversity and negativity from others, summed up so well in the words of this song by Labi Siffre.
"The higher you build your barriers
The taller I become
The further you take my rights away
The faster I will run
You can deny me, you can decide
To turn your face away
No matter 'cause there's
Something inside so strong
I know that I can make it"
My light will shine so brightly it will blind you   *"So Strong" Labi Siffre*

Stolen Years

What you have been through makes you unique. Maybe there are regrets with the way things have taken course; you might feel that the years have been stolen from you. But there may be real positives as well. It may be that you wouldn't have met certain people, had certain opportunities or discovered certain things about yourself without experiencing the difficulties.

Maybe you feel angry that time has been taken up with ill health, depression and it is natural to grieve for the losses you have incurred. The key is to not allow sadness and resentment to impinge on the here and now as that in turn allows your future to be stolen as well!

A friend of ours, Louise Pratt offered the poem below, written following this conversation with her father;

–"I was talking to my parents, quite sadly, wondering and imagining who and where I'd have been now if I had not had a sizable portion of my adult working life stolen from me. I had new vigour and enthusiasm for work and life, but what would I have achieved? I enquired."

My father proudly and quite simply replied saying 'Who knows? But I do know that you would not be the person you are today".

Hopes and dreams to face together,
Man and wife to be forever.
A child to watch and to care for,
The plans to expand, to have one more.
To be able to work and to play,
A zest for each and every day.
A place to call our very own,
Building a house into a home.
Friends and family that hold us dear,
Our love we share to have them near.
Working hard to achieve our goal,
Putting in our heart and soul.

One day this is there to be snatched away,
It's going to be a price to pay.
I am now the one who is ill,
Will we be able to swallow the bitter pill?
Hope fades and our soul is weak,
Our life is tested and cures we seek.
I miss the sound of laughter once more,
I look no further to the vision I saw.
My role as mother, wife and daughter,
Feels threatened as a lamb to slaughter.

Am I seen and heard as me,
When looking what do they see?
My daughter I love but cannot hold,
These are the best days I am told.
My house, my prison, it was meant to be home,
I was in this shell with shadows alone.
My friends, the fun that was there to share,
Going out is now too much to bear.
My husband had to be all and one,
Where was our passion, desire had gone.

My job, my rewards were going to plan,
They matter no more to my working life span.
Louise

It is natural to wonder how things could have been, but futile to let regrets impinge on the present. Or, as they say, shit happens! The biggest revenge on people who have treated you badly or experiences of life which were unpleasant is simple – to be happy!

Louise is now enjoying life working with people who have learning disabilities and who experience mental distress.

"My life now, well firstly it's so far removed from my past inner world that I often have to pinch myself to see if it's for real. How? The first thing that hits me is that the past has earned its place as just a distant memory. No more snatches of dark thoughts, flashbacks, despair and desperation.
This was not only due to my distress, but also due to the effects of treatment, all in the name of care in the Twentieth Century.

I can only now look back objectively and use my experiences in a positive light. How is my life better now? It feels like living in a world that I belong to, I realise I have had to work hard to prove my new existence and this is usually about other people's fears not just my own. I have regained a recognised status again in society by saying 'I do this job', 'I belong to this group'; 'I believe in this' and 'this is my life'.

I have had to learn to live, function, feel and believe again. I had to reconnect to those things and people that had not entered my inner world with me. I had to re-establish relationships that had been wounded by my isolation. I had to believe in myself when no-one else did and I had to allow myself to experience relapses with the knowledge that this was to be accepted to myself and others.

There was nothing to physically identify me as someone who was experiencing mental distress then, and now, there is nothing to show the world of my past experiences, but I live my life with new meaning and enthusiasm that shows in all I endeavour to do, with the people I meet and the actions I take, so that my legacy from the past can reflect my life with new meaning, and in every detail, to who I can now be".
Louise Pratt

Do you feel that psychic distress has contributed to certain things being stolen from you?
Can you work out the specifics or is it just a vague feeling?
How do you feel about your losses?

It may help to talk this over with a friend to identify what you feel is missing. When you come to an understanding, then ask yourself what can you do to take you forward?

I am very happy
Because I have conquered myself
And not the world.

I am very happy
Because I have loved the world
And not myself.

I am very happy
Because I have not surrendered
Either to the world or to myself.
Sri Chinmoy "The Divine Hero", Published by Watkins

10 things to do before I die

Some years ago a relative was told she had terminal cancer and a very short time to live. She wrote a list of things which she had never had the opportunity to do but had always wanted to, and family and friends supported her in achieving everything on the wish list. In her final days she undoubtedly lived live to the full.

It is difficult to imagine how we would feel if told our time here was about to be cut short. What would be our priorities? What would we regret?

The following thoughts are from Emma Bombeck, written after she found out she was dying from cancer.
"If I had my life to live over…………"
I would have talked less and listened more

I would have taken the time to listen to my grandfather ramble about his youth
I would never have insisted the car windows be rolled up on a summer day because my hair had just been teased and sprayed
I would have sat on the lawn with my children and not worried about grass stains
I would never have bought anything because it was practical, wouldn't show the dirt or was guaranteed to last a lifetime
I would have cried and laughed less while watching television and more while watching life

She sums up by saying,
"Stop sweating the small stuff. Don't worry about who doesn't like you, who has more, or who's doing what. Instead let's cherish the relationships we have and those we have with us who do love us. Let's think about what God has blessed us with. And what we are doing each day to promote ourselves mentally, physically, emotionally as well as spiritually."

What would be on your wish list of things to do before you die?
Write down ten things that you would love to do (or see) before you die.

Are you able to put them in order of priority or in order of likelihood of them happening?
If you could choose just one of them to happen which would it be?

What stops you from achieving that one thing? (Or at least planning or working towards it)
How would you feel if you reached the end of your life and had not attempted to achieve that one thing?

"Dance like nobody's watching;
Love like you've never been hurt.
Sing like nobody's listening;
Live like it's heaven on earth."
Mark Twain

"Avoiding danger is no safer in the long run than outright exposure; life is either a daring adventure or nothing" **……..and I like adventures!**
Helen Keller

Chapter 9
The THRIVE© Approach
Emancipation

"Emancipate yourselves from mental slavery;
None but ourselves can free our minds.
Have no fear for atomic energy,
cause none of them can stop the time.
                    Bob Marley – Redemption Song

Emancipation is liberation, release, freeing somebody or yourself from restriction. Disingenuously the importance of power, lack of power and psychic distress is never openly acknowledged by society. The very act of moving on in your life, reclaiming, recovering and fighting back is a political act. The singular medicalisation of distress, "It's simply a disturbance in your neuro amines" has been one of the greatest follies of modern times because it removes the personal meaning and responsibility from the equation. This position is not against the use of medicine in distress, indeed medicine can be one way of coping, but it doesn't cure.

Put simply, how can you cure trauma, life events or your loss of dreams with a pill? How can neuro-surgery cure sexual abuse? You will always have been abused with or without meds or surgery. Offering these things as cures is our bugbear as all they could ever do is alter you and your reaction to these events. You were still traumatised - you just don't care about it any more, but you don't care about anything else either! And there may be significant long term side effects from just taking the drugs.

It is important to construct your own view of your psychic distress and to find clarity on your context for the experiences. Knowing how you view your experiences, constructing your own explanations and finding your own route to accepting and resolving the distress is not only emancipatory but can also make the difference between being seen as mad or being understood by others.

Taking control, finding your own way, developing your own meaning and understanding and becoming a victor not a victim is a key to moving on. It is hard to emancipate yourself in Europe because of many factors. Stigma, social welfare that reinforces and relies on a sickness and disability model, social expectations - all have their parts to play. These are the things we will guide you through here. The very act of getting through this chapter is a political act! We are neither of us revolutionaries but we both recognise that personal and social politics are crucial if you are to thrive. Recognise this and if possible use your knowledge to reclaim your future.

"They said that I was mad, I said that it were they who were mad
Damn them, they outvoted me!
                    Nathaniel Lee (the mad poet)

Don't fight a losing battle

Many people we have known when they move along their road to recovery become very angry about how they have been treated, the denial of their experiences and the undervaluing of their opinions and expertise in their own lives. Often, this anger can be further pathologised as some psychiatrists can even turn that into a symptom. They can try to over rule you and say that they know better, increasing medication when you ask for a reduction. This increases anger and leads to a vicious circle. Marion found that for her just being assertive not aggressive led to threats to increase medication!

Once you become intricated into the psychiatric system almost everything you do is in danger of being pathologised and seen as a symptom of ill health rather than an expression of your individual personality. This can often lead to "fighting" the system; how do you prove you are sane when everything around you is crazy?

DL Rosenhan, in an inspirational paper in the 1970's got himself and a group of psychology students admitted to various psychiatric hospitals by pretending to hear voices. After this admission they never again pretended anything, answered questions truthfully and were their normal selves. There were many conclusions from this study, for instance, none of them were detected as impostors, all were defined as insane and their behaviour i.e. writing notes was turned into a symptom - "writing behaviour".

When the people disclosed themselves as impostors they were not believed and were told they may indeed be students but they were also actually mentally ill, they just didn't know it! All of them were detected as impostors very quickly by the other patients. Rosenhan's key conclusion from this study was that we can't differentiate between sanity and insanity. Once diagnosed as ill all that you do, no matter how normal, is construed as a sign of madness.

Choose where to fight and when – fight clever! Obviously we are speaking metaphorically here, but in a political game, you really have to behave cleverly. Don't stop taking meds when you have people interfering in your life. If you want to stop taking psychiatric medication, get advice. Find someone who you trust and will be honest with you, visit our website and read about others experiences of the pitfalls of stopping meds and also the advantages of being drug free, and read some of the literature such as Peter Lehmann's book "Coming off Psychiatric Drugs" available on line at http://www.peter-lehmann-publishing.com.

Find allies, friends or workers who will help you and support your decisions. Our colleague, Jorn, is a manager of a Recovery and rehabilitation service in Denmark. One of his clients wished to come off her drugs and asked for his support. When she started to withdraw she became animated to the point of mania – her workers panicked, Jorn simply told them to "stay with her" and "see her through". She cut her hair – they panicked even more. He simply said, "See it through". In a few weeks she had returned to her own sense of being, had overcome the difficult phase and was rejoicing in the fact that she was drug free, back to herself. It would have been very easy for him to cave in and stop the process. That would have been through his own fears, not hers. Instead she feels emancipated, ready to move on and discover new life.

Recognising the importance of you as you is a vital part of the emancipation process. Be psychotic and proud. Maybe you are someone who has been abused, but come through as a victor. You maybe a voice hearer, someone who happens to have self injured or still does, but whatever the distress and behaviour linked to it, this is a fragment of self – a microcosm of who you truly are.

Know and believe in your rights. If you do feel intimidated in speaking out and asserting what you need, engage others to help you. Take power around you, take control of you. Raise your own expectations of yourself. A British psychologist, Rufus May was diagnosed with schizophrenia and told he would need to take medication the rest of his life.

"After the third admission I was more wary of the risks of medication withdrawal. However six months later, having successfully left home, I was finding it a struggle to have enough energy to work part-time and also go to art school. I decided to stop taking the medication against medical advice, effectively disengaging with mental health services fourteen months after my initial contact. Since then I have not taken any neuroleptic medication. I have done various jobs before deciding to go back into the mental health system as a clinical psychologist. I think my recovery occurred despite rather than because of my psychiatric treatment. I believe I narrowly escaped a permanent "sick role" as a schizophrenic."

Professor Marius Romme, is a highly respected psychiatrist renowned for his innovative work on voice hearing and his simple humanity. He is outspoken in his criticism of medicalised psychiatry and it's pseudo-labelling. He remains firm in his belief that many people, like Rufus May, recover due to their own innate abilities and the support from friends and family rather than from the psychiatric interventions they receive. He states,

"People who recover do this outside psychiatry. We have often met people who recover from these mental health problems and diagnosis, but they did that outside psychiatry. They started in psychiatric care, either in or outside psychiatric hospitals but became rather angry with the care they received"

He goes on to say that there was no interest in the distress people experienced during psychosis; rather the focus was on the symptoms not on the way in which people were suffering and the diagnostic procedure did not help them in any way to solve their problems; it more or less denied their human needs, of making sense of what happened to them. They were never asked what had happened to them in daily life in connection with the experience, and demoralizing statements were made about the consequences of their diagnosis, for example that they would have to take medicine all their life, have to adapt to the illness and expect less possibilities in life. The medication did not help, but doctors stuck to the idea that the person needed them nevertheless.

"This angriness seemed to motivate the patient to try to take his life in his own hands again or go looking elsewhere to be helped more successfully. But in mental health care it was often seen as part of the illness. Although anger is not a symptom of schizophrenia, it was interpreted as lack of insight into their illness, a quite disempowering interpretation. We generally find that people who adapt to the psychiatric care system have less chance of recovery than people who protest against it and also plan in their own way". Professor Marius Romme

Ron Coleman a writer of many emancipatory works such as "The Politics of the Madhouse" and "Recovery an Alien Concept" rather succinctly asserts that *"within the realms of psychiatric practice it is accepted that the most powerful practitioner is the psychiatrist. Their power is rooted not only in the authority given to them by the state, but also in their singular right to make diagnosis. It is this ownership of a supposed expert knowledge that gives them so much power over their clients. I would contend that the real expert of the client's experience is the client and it is they, not the psychiatrist, who own the knowledge that makes recovery a possibility".*

Do you recognise that you are an expert in your own experience?
You know what it feels like, maybe even have a context for where the experience originates; most importantly you know what helps you and what does not.

Reclaiming your future may involve some reassessment of who you have become and how things have evolved for you. Sometimes it is good to take stock of the positives that have come out of despair and despondency, and remind ourselves that although we are different to how we were prior to mental health difficulties we have grown and developed through adversity.

Consider the following;

I think differently about what is important in life.

I have a greater appreciation for the value of my own life.

I have developed new interests.

I have gained new skills

I have a greater feeling of self-reliance.

I have become a stronger person.

I have a better understanding of spiritual matters

I know who my true friends are.

I have made new friendships.

I am more willing to express my emotions.

I know better that I can handle difficulties

I am able to do better things with my life.

I am better able to accept the way things work out.

I can better appreciate each day.

Which statements most accurately reflect how you view your recovery journey? It may be useful for you to write a short account of your recovery journey so far, indeed some people find it very therapeutic to see in black and white how far they have travelled, and some of the more positive experiences that have arisen from experiencing psychic distress.

Participation

Many individuals would assert that participation is critical to their recovery and evidence from literature supports this claim. Participating in making decisions regarding one's mental health is the common thread amongst service users who live well in the presence or absence of symptoms associated with distress. It is important that you find your own definition of living well and what works for you. This, then, brings emancipation. Participation in defining one's own journey either unaided or in alliance with mental health workers can increase your sense of achievement and power.

Empowerment

Empowerment – or rather taking power is an important component of emancipation.
We are not of the belief that anyone can empower you, i.e. give you power, but that it is something you claim for yourself. By feeling in control and having power in your life, this will enable you to grow and develop as a person with a sense of worth and self esteem. Others can be important in sowing the seeds whereby you can reclaim what is yours, but they cannot do it for you.

It might be useful to look at the following lists to determine how "empowered" you currently feel or what you need to accomplish for yourself.

These are some of the things you might experience as empowering (within the psychiatric system and in your interactions with friends and family)

- Being listened to – and action taken as a result
- Being "heard"
- No fear of consequences for speaking your mind!
- Good communication between yourself and others
- Working at your pace
- Not feeling pressured
- Being consulted
- Treated as an equal
- Making your own decisions
- Not being judged
- Taking responsibility for your own actions
- Having real choices
- Being valued for being you!
- Being respected
- Able to progress
- Receiving understanding and empathy
- Able to weigh up and take risks
- A sense of achievement

What other things sum up empowerment for you?

Write a plan.
Say what helps and why, and include how you are able to manage the following;

- **Asserting your beliefs and frame of reference**
- **Valuing yourself**
- **Building self esteem**
- **Being fair to yourself**
- **Being more objective about your good qualities**
- **Feeling better about yourself**
- **Being more confident in your abilities**
- **Being calm when you think about yourself and your future**
- **Thinking more positively**

What can you do to make sure that you begin to take power again?

Personal responsibility

It is our responsibility to make our lives as good as they can be, our own determination that shapes and generally directs the journey. Often this is forgotten and other people blamed when things go wrong. Recovery requires self examination, self accountability and a willingness to stand up as an individual against injustices. Other people may interfere and as we've seen in the section on interdependence we may have to compromise, but we are responsible primarily for ourselves and we can change aspects of ourselves.

Happiness and good mental health requires an investment – effort, participation and resourcefulness. It is not simply handed to you, it does require work and commitment but many people who have come through mental ill health speak of the rewards of such hard work outweighing the effort.

Be yourself

Although there is still a degree of stigma surrounding anyone who has had psychic distress (the press are notoriously bad in their coverage) and some ignorance from those who have not had first hand experience, there is growing awareness and a realisation that "There but for the grace of God go I!"

1 in 4 people experience psychic distress each year and it is only by shrugging off the ignorance, being proud of coming through your experiences, reminding yourself of your worth and value and standing up proud that can influence others' negativity. Be happy being yourself! It is much better to be you than to pretend to be someone else. Accept that we are just human and forget trying to be perfect in the eyes of others. In many cultures there is no taboo, no stigma regarding what are after all, human frailties. What you have come through has made you YOU!

What's your label?

We have noticed that some people who use psychiatric services often greet newcomers at meetings or conferences with an introduction of their name followed by diagnosis, "Hi, I'm Joe, I'm a Schizophrenic" or "I'm Katy, I have Bi-polar Disorder". Whilst this could be seen as empowering themselves by being "Psychotic and proud" it is rather disconcerting, limiting and is only an illusory step of taking power. It would seem that their "illness" is the part of their psyche they most relate to.

111

We would argue that the labels are arbitrary anyway, say little about you other than in a narrow, medicalised way and reinforces the myth that there is a sector of society – psychiatrists and mental health professionals who have reached a consensus of agreement as to what constitutes illnesses such as "schizophrenia" and therefore how to treat it.

In her book, "Schizophrenia, a Scientific Delusion?" clinical psychologist, Mary Boyle challenges and questions the scientific status of the concept of schizophrenia. She emphasises that this is not to deny the existence of bizarre behaviour or the distress it may cause, but that it is necessary to ask searching questions about the labelling of some behaviour as symptomatic of mental illness. *"It is unlikely that constructive alternatives to "Schizophrenia" will be developed unless we face not only the deficiencies of the concept but also the social and intellectual habits which have allowed it to flourish".*

If we have to construct a disorder to support and help people in distress perhaps the more generic label of "Post Traumatic Stress Disorder" might be more appropriate, or to simply say that people are "in crisis, or psychic distress"

How many psychiatric labels are in existence? Too many for us to include here, certainly, and each year sees the invention of dozens more. What does the label actually mean? The short answer, very little! A diagnostic label merely groups a certain set of symptoms at a certain time, says nothing of the origins of the experiences, the personal meaning and most importantly says nothing about how to live and cope with the experiences or to surmount them. Understanding the way diagnoses are arrived at and agreed upon and having some knowledge of the political clout and influence of the pharmaceutical industry and its oppressive marketing structures can inform the way you regard your own mental distress.

Often within psychiatry the terms as to what constitutes normal behaviour are dictated. A body of "experts" (American Psychiatric Association committee members) determine what is "acceptable" or "unacceptable. Unlike medical diagnoses that convey a probable cause, appropriate treatment and likely prognosis, the disorders listed in DSM 4 and ICD 10 are terms arrived at through peer consensus. Is this a meaningful way of looking at distress? It's less than helpful when psychiatry represents a rather narrow image of normality, applying an illness label in a formal manner to many variations of being. *"Just because we put a name to it doesn't mean we understand it"* Mike

"We have known for quite some time that the concept of schizophrenia has no scientific validity. We now however have an alternative which is more helpful. It is time to challenge the old concept and leave it behind. The old concept is harmful because, it is impossible to solve the problems of the patient diagnosed with this illness.

We not only know that the symptoms exist and the illness does not, but we now know more about where the symptoms come from. It is a false suggestion that the symptoms are the result of an underlying illness. They are partly a reaction to serious problems in the life of the person and partly a reaction towards other symptoms. Therefore attention should be given to the reality for the patient of his or her complaints and the background for each of them should be explored. Only then do we discover what the problems for the patient are, and only then might we be able to help solve those problems" **Marius Romme, Emeritus Professor of Social Psychiatry**

Jacqui Dillon, National Chair of the UK Hearing Voices Network states,

'In our experience, gained through more than 15 years running a national network, listening to people who hear voices, many of them living with a diagnosis of schizophrenia; it is clear that there is a definite link between traumatic life events and psychosis. On a daily basis, we hear terrible stories of sexual, emotional and physical abuse, and the impact of racism, poverty, neglect and stigma on peoples' lives.

We do not seek to reduce people to a set of symptoms that we wish to suppress and control with medication. We show respect for the reality of the trauma they have endured and bear witness to the suffering they have experienced.

We honour peoples' resilience and capacity to survive, often against the odds. The reduction of peoples distressing life experiences into a diagnosis of schizophrenia means that they are condemned to lives dulled by drugs and blighted by stigma and offered no opportunity to make sense of their experiences. Their routes to recovery are hindered.

Rather than pathologising individuals, we have a collective responsibility to people who have experienced abuse, to acknowledge the reality and impact of those experiences and to support them to get the help they need. Abuse thrives in secrecy. We must expose the truth and not perpetuate injustice further; otherwise today's child abuse victims become tomorrow's psychiatric patients."

Are you knowledgeable about your own distress?

Do you believe the pseudoscience that some professionals use? Particularly damaging may be the messages sent out by so many that psychic distress is simply a biochemical imbalance which can only be managed by medication. This is a theory, rather than fact, but one that is widely presented as the uncontested truth.

It is, in truth, difficult for the average person to contend this. Within the system, consultant psychiatrists hold vast amounts of power. They are used to employing this power unchallenged. The old joke being, "What's the difference between God and a psychiatrist? Well, God doesn't think he's a psychiatrist!"

We firmly believe that the individual who has experienced psychic distress is the expert of their own experience, and thankfully there are significant numbers of nurses, mental health workers and psychiatrists who also contribute to that principle and speak out openly to challenge the myths that still abound. Statistical research over the years prove that psychic distress relates directly to trauma, and anecdotal evidence from workers supports this.

Part of the emancipation process may well be developing the skills and ability to sort out the truth from the psychobollocks. Empowering yourself through reading a wide range of literature, looking at the bigger picture, knowing yourself and your difficulties will all contribute to developing a rounded knowledge and awareness so that you can then decide what you require (or not) from professional workers.

Rejoice – you are not alone!
If you have experienced mental health problems you are in excellent company – that of some of the greatest artists, playwrights, composers, poets, scientists, architects throughout the world.
All of these people have suffered mental health problems

Isaac Newton	**Leonard Cohen**	**T.S. Eliot**
Martin Luther	**Sheryl Crow**	**Emily Dickinson**
Friedrich Nietzche	**Nick Drake**	**William Blake**
Oliver Cromwell	**Jeff Buckley**	**John Keats**
Mahatma Gandhi	**Eric Clapton**	**Sylvia Plath**
William Pitt	**Marilyn Monroe**	**Sergei Rachmaninoff**
Theodore Roosevelt	**Robin Williams**	**Richard Wagner**
Napoleon Bonaparte	**Spike Milligan**	**Irving Berlin**
Winston Churchill	**Hans Christian Anderson**	**Cole Porter**
Yitzhak Rabin	**Agatha Christie**	**Ludwig von Beethoven**
Vincent van Gogh	**John Bunyan**	**Gustav Holst**
Paul Gauguin	**Charles Dickens**	**Franz Liszt**
Rembrandt van Rijn	**Graham Greene**	**Stephen Fry**
Edward Lear	**Ernest Hemingway**	**Angelina Jolie**
Michelangelo	**Eugene O'Neill**	**Courtney Love**
Jackson Pollock	**Tennessee Williams**	
Edvard Munch	**Robert Burns**	
Ray Charles	**Lord Byron**	

"Some years ago in psychosis I entertained the idea that my friends had arranged a secret party with Spike Milligan as the guest of honour. Imagine my disappointment when, as I was led into hospital to be sectioned, the realisation dawned that there was no party, no Spike, just doctors, nurses and a syringe waiting. A couple of years later, however, I wrote to him and he responded to my letter by agreeing to give a poetry reading at the mental health project I had set up. I got to personally escort him from his home to the project and finally we had our party!" Marion

Where did you start seeing gnomes, Mr Milligan?"
"In India", said Spike. "They came out in the hot weather".
"How were they dressed?"
"From head to foot and sometimes backwards"
The inspector wrote it all down laboriously.
"I see. When did you stop seeing them?"
"When I stopped believing in them"   *"Surviving Spike Milligan"- John Antrobus*

"Normalising" your life
Spike's way of dealing with his depression, he said, was just to go with it, go to bed until he felt able to get up and get on with it. His friends and family accepted this. Having the power to act on what you know you need is very empowering and when others around you accept you as you are it is very reaffirming to mental wellbeing. During our years of working with people we are always impressed with the range of coping strategies people employ to counteract the problems they face.

Many people use the technique of speaking into a mobile phone when responding to their voices. It allows access to any public place without looking mad!

Consider the following questions
1. How are you spending your time?
2. Do you have a balance of non mental health related things and people?
3. What do you take pleasure in?
4. What helps create feelings of mastery?
5. What would you like to do more of but find it difficult to do?
6. What do you not like to do?
7. What do significant people in your life want you to do more often?

It can be all too easy to become immersed in psychic distress to the point where "normal" life doesn't exist – just trips to clinics, day centres, hospitals and user groups! This is a form of institutionalisation which takes over unless we're careful.

Many people find solace and support from these things but true emancipation comes with the realisation that in fact it is these things which hold us back and put us in a box. Peeling back layers from being institutionalised is difficult. Psychic distress creates a paradoxical situation for many people – the support often required to nurture us back to health – mental health professionals, treatments, specialist services, day centres etc. can ultimately be the very thing which binds us and maintains through its institutionalising nature, leaving us fearful of a life independent of these people and situations which may have helped in the past.

How, then, can the balance be created? After all many strong friendships, activities you enjoy and areas of support will remain in the domain of mental health. It is our personal attitudes that make the difference and remove the institutionalised persona. Changing from the person who previously "couldn't" because of mental ill health to the person who not only "can" but "does" regardless of difficulties is the key. As explained in an earlier chapter, we can choose to remove ourselves from the prison.

Emancipation or liberation comes with taking control of one's own life and celebrating your own individuality and uniqueness. Playing a vital role in society and being valued can enhance our sense of freedom and remove us from the constraints of being regarded as mentally unwell, being maintained in the system and feeling that "life" is something which happens for other people.

Part of personal growth, knowledge and empowerment comes with redefining and reframing not just the experiences you have had, but also the terminology that you choose to accept and utilise. Consider the difference in meaning and inference between Care plans and Recovery plans, a mentally ill person or someone who has experienced mental ill health.

There is a subtle yet dynamic distinction. Choosing to focus on mental wellness not illness, dismissing the labels, taking pride in self as an individual, taking responsibility for actions – all of these things will enhance the emancipation process.

Psychological studies indicate that some people who have experienced physical or psychological problems would go so far as to say that their quality of life following their problems is actually enhanced and more satisfying than it was prior to the problems occurring. Whilst not everyone may take this view, it is undoubtedly true that strength of character and fortitude and the acquisition of a more helpful life perspective emerge as inherent qualities. Or in simple terms you learn not to "sweat over the small stuff!"

Research also indicates that it is people who seek non materialistic goals who are happiest in life. Perhaps overcoming mental distress and despair forces us to re-examine our values and sort out what really matters in our lives and strive for happiness, health and fulfilment.

"Don't hurry, don't worry.
You're only here for a short visit.
So be sure to stop and smell the flowers"
Walter Hagen

My personal rights
We are all entitled to basic human rights, though some would assert that at times psychiatric services systematically strip away many rights. Once a person is detained in a psychiatric hospital on a section there are obvious rights that get taken away, not least freedom and choice of treatment.

But there are other more subtle ways in which services restrict people's freedom and rights. People who have been abused often state that the system punishes them again by not understanding their complex needs relating to the abuse, is quick to see all "unusual" behaviour as manipulative, attention seeking and maladaptive. Many young people who have been abused end up in cyclical situations of being maintained, medicated, released without the problems being resolved only to find themselves in a "revolving door" situation.

The THRIVE© approach is our attempt to encourage individuals, their families, supporters and workers to break traditional cycles by thinking in different ways, looking at sustaining people through crisis rather than maintaining them and fostering institutionalisation. One way to support people is to recognise their needs and their rights, and to encourage rather than discourage autonomy.

People who have been abused often have many of their human rights violated when they are young, and on reaching adulthood they are not used to standing up for their own rights. Some adults, abused as children, may not even consider that they have the same basic rights as other adults, but no matter what you think about yourself, you are entitled to your basic rights as a human.

You have the right to;

- Say no to things you do not wish to do or are detrimental to you

- Physical, emotional and spiritual safety

- The right to take pride in your achievements, abilities and successes

- To feel appreciated, and not used

- To be treated respectfully

- To be able to express your opinions, feelings and thoughts openly without judgement

- To have choices and make your own decisions

- To have your support needs met

- To have the freedom to be an individual

Having a Voice

It may be as you recover from psychic distress and become stronger that you wish to have a say in how services could be improved for others not quite so far along their journey. This can be empowering, but we also need to point out here that the mental health arena is highly political, often dogmatic and sadly all too often tokenistic. Mental Health Trusts throughout the country are notorious for engaging with a few well chosen individuals or groups, often excluding independent and more radical voices.

Therefore to persevere and have real voice takes courage, strength and determination, is often unpaid and can be personally challenging. However many committed individuals continue to involve themselves and retain their integrity, working with and on behalf of service users rather than becoming "professional User Trust representatives" and toeing the party line.

The common denominator for those working for change is to improve services for all. Psychic distress is no discriminator – it can affect any one of us at any time, or our families or our friends.

Speaking Out

It is incredibly difficult for survivors of the mental health system to critique the system in which they have received health care, but for those who do it is mainly borne of a passion to change things for the better for those who follow, for the same mistakes not to be repeated and to sow the seeds of change. So it is vital that those who are more empowered and can speak out do so in meaningful ways to help those without such a voice.

> *"First they came for the Jews*
> *and I did not speak out*
> *because I was not a Jew.*
> *Then they came for the Communists*
> *and I did not speak out*
> *because I was not a Communist.*
> *Then they came for the trade unionists*
> *and I did not speak out*
> *because I was not a trade unionist.*
> *Then they came for me*
> *and there was no one left*
> *to speak out for me".*
>
> *Pastor Martin Niemöller*

Helping others – service users as workers?

If you wish to help others move on and want to become involved in various aspects of mental health work, e.g. attending policy meetings, running support groups, delivering expert by experience training it can be challenging but also proves very therapeutic for all parties concerned. People in distress may gain hope and comfort in talking to someone "who has been there". Studies show that the therapeutic relationship is of vastly more importance than the therapy itself. Qualities such as empathy, understanding, respect, active listening and congruence will move people on, the actual content being secondary to these values of working.

"In our own woundedness we can become a source of life for others" Henri Nouwen

Being able to articulate your experiences to others, and sharing expertise with workers to inform their good practice will increase your confidence and take you even further in your recovery, informing and enhancing your spiritual journey.

Articulation

"The man who can articulate the movements of his inner life, who can give names to his varied experiences need no longer be a victim of himself, but is able slowly and consistently to remove the obstacles that prevent the spirit from entering" Henri Nouwen

Sometimes a component of psychic distress is feeling that you are alone and unable to articulate that distress adequately to express to others what you are experiencing. Many people have found comfort in being able to share stories with others who have been there and eventually give a name, expression or description to what is the problem.

Being able to be of help to others has proven the final step to recovery for many individuals who have experienced psychic distress. Some would go so far as to say the help received this way – joining user groups, sharing stories and problems was far more beneficial than anything that services could offer.

Contemplation

Distance from the psychic distress you have experienced allows a perspective of contemplation which in turn can lead to wisdom, having come through the flames. Many people speak of re-evaluating their lives, knowing what is truly meaningful and of worth. Some go so far as to say they prefer the people they have become through adversity.

"The contemplative is guided by a vision of what he has seen beyond the trivial concerns of a possessive world. He knows that he is considered by many as a fool, a madman, and a danger to society and a threat to mankind. The contemplative critic takes away the illusory mask of the manipulative world and has the courage to show what the true situation is. More than anything else he will look for signs of hope and promise in the situation in which he finds himself. The contemplative critic has the sensibility to notice the smallest mustard seed and the trust to believe that "When it is grown it is the biggest shrub of all and becomes a tree so that the birds of the air come and shelter in its branches" Henri Nouwen

Advance directives

If you are unable at this stage to emancipate yourself from services, one way in which you may choose to empower yourself is to take responsibility for your future healthcare. An advance directive is a way of making your wishes and views known or making informed choices about treatment, at some future time. Doctors and other healthcare workers must usually take these wishes (advance statements) into account and cannot normally give you treatment without your consent. If you are incapable of consenting, they can treat you according to how they see your 'best interests'. However, the courts have confirmed that if you set out your wishes in advance they will be valid at the time treatment is being considered. There are, however limits to what an advance directive can do;

An advance directive cannot compel a doctor to give you a particular type of treatment. This is a clinical decision and may also be influenced by other factors such as financial considerations. An advance directive can only be used to direct what treatment you do not wish to have. Legally, an advance directive does not have to be in writing. However, a written statement is preferable as it helps to avoid any doubt about what you intend. An advance directive needs to be carefully drafted so that its terms are clear. It does not need to use specific language, but it must be obvious what treatment you are refusing or consenting to have, and in what circumstances. An advance directive must cover the particular circumstances which arise. For example, it should cover possible advances in drug treatment to which you might wish to consent, otherwise a blanket refusal of medication would mean that you would not be given the new drugs.

The statement should include your name, address, the date it was drafted and your signature. You should also include a statement in the document to the effect that you understand what you are doing and have the necessary legal capacity to make such a directive. There is no legal requirement to have your signature witnessed but it is a good idea to have your statement signed by someone who will be able to say that you were mentally competent at the time you made it and understood what you were doing. You may want the support of an advocate or advice from a lawyer.

It is important that your advance directive is entered into your medical notes so that in an emergency it is found and acted upon. You should therefore send a copy to your GP and to any hospital which is treating you (or has done so recently). Copies of your directive should also be sent to other important people who may be consulted over your treatment such as your nearest relative. Your advance directive will come into effect if and when you lose the capacity to make decisions about your treatment. Until that time you can make the decisions yourself without reference to any written statement prepared in advance.

Emancipation from the system

As you begin to take more control of your life you may come to the realization that services are not necessary to you at all and that true recovery will involve emancipating yourself by completely removing yourself from the psychiatric system. This will require you taking ownership of your experiences, accepting responsibility for your wellbeing and sustaining yourself through the lows that may still arise from time to time. But remember, you have come a long way – you have all the skills, it's just having the confidence to utilize them!

> *I teetered on the edge of doom, degenerate and broken*
> *I learnt how to sustain myself in storms*
> *Scoured and stripped of all pretence, shorn of all illusion*
> *I learnt how to sustain myself in storms*
> *The Waterboys "Sustain"*

Only you can know if and when that is right for you. It is certainly difficult to give up a "sick role" when usually the sicker you prove to be the more you gain financially in terms of Disability Living Allowance and health related benefits. But it is worth considering and balancing the non financial benefits to you reclaiming your life.

The THRIVE© Approach
Final Thoughts

Live your life not your label

Many of the people we meet who have shrugged off their illness tag have repeatedly stated the case for doing so and would say that the benefits of taking a valued role in society, feeling a sense of pride and achievement in their recovery, a self worth that comes from surviving trauma and coming out the other end is far more meaningful than anything of monetary value. Many people have also commented on how much stronger they have become as a result of their psychic distress and journey back to wellness.

"I'm so glad that this has taken me so long, coz it's the journey that made me so strong".
"Warmer Climate" Snow Patrol

No one can walk your particular journey; each person's route is individual and unique. But you can give yourself the choice to live within the limits of the label given to you, or to ignore the constraints that some people may try to place upon you. In order to experience the richness and totality of life it necessitates encompassing the lows as well as the highs –this often proves to be far more personally rewarding than simply existing at an intermediary level, staying "in the box" ascribed to you.

From psychic distress to emancipation

The following extract was written by our colleague, Olga Runciman who was, effectively "written off" by psychiatric services and told in no uncertain terms that she would never work again! Olga, a qualified nurse now works as a recovery consultant in Copenhagen and is chair of the Danish Hearing Voices Network

"A psychiatric diagnosis which smashes your life, resulting in the loss of friends, work, studies, money, maybe even your home, not to mention the loss of respect, the stigmatization and the alienation that one now faces from the outside world is devastating. After the initial shock and if one is unable to find, or get the help that is necessary to recover, and instead receives treatment imposed by a psychiatric system that thinks and often insists they know what is best, resignation steps in.

It can be very difficult to hold on to one's dignity, self-respect and self-worth in a world which no longer accepts you as a positive member of society. And so it can be easy, maybe even tempting to accept ones diagnosis and use it as a prop to give some kind of meaning for why one is where one is. But precisely because of that, it can be very difficult to let go of it.

The consequences of the diagnosis have been so devastating that if one starts to realize that it is just a name and says nothing about who one is, about one's life and the circumstances that have led to the situation one now is in, then one inevitably has to ask "What then was I doing the last however many years?"

I am not alone in having been caught in such a cycle in a system which though kind in a patronizing patriarchal way did not listen and stripped me of myself, disempowered me, giving pills saying it was biochemical when it so obviously was trauma. This resulted in a permanent feeling that I was a living dead person. When I realized that this feeling was not a symptom but actually quite true in the spiritual sense, I realized I had two choices, either to go all the way and die, or grab life by freeing myself. I chose the latter.

To free yourself, to let go, to grab life and live it to its fullest potential is the greatest gift you can give yourself… and those you touch. For who knows maybe your fight for emancipation will be the start of a fundamental change within society".

Your future is unwritten, ready for you to decide which route you take, which person you decide you will be. Psychic distress may only be the start of the journey. Emancipation may be a huge and difficult step for you to take, but what is the alternative? Today may be where your book begins.

"I am unwritten, can't read my mind, I'm undefined
I'm just beginning, the pen's in my hand, ending unplanned

Staring at the blank page before you
Open up the dirty window
Let the sun illuminate the words that you could not find

Reaching for something in the distance
So close you can almost taste it
Release your innovations
Feel the rain on your skin
No one else can feel it for you
Only you can let it in
No one else, no one else
Can speak the words on your lips
Drench yourself in words unspoken
Live your life with arms wide open
Today is where your book begins
The rest is still unwritten"
"Unwritten" Natasha Bedingfield

Come on you boy child, you winner and loser
Come on you miner for truth and delusion
And shine!
"Shine on you crazy diamond" Pink Floyd

Sometimes it's just a different perspective that is needed

Look sideways, if you don't believe us

If you have enjoyed this book, benefited in any small way, if it has set you thinking and you wish
to respond please contact us via our website
www.crazydiamond.org.uk
Or email us
Mikesvoice@aol.com
Marionaslan@aol.com